Talk about the Valley

Norman Creighton

Edited by Hilary Sircom

NIMBUS
PUBLISHING

Copyright © Hilary Sircom, 2001

All rights reserved. No part of this book may be reproduced, stored in a retrieval system or transmitted in any form or by any means without the prior written permission from the publisher, or, in the case of photocopying or other reprographic copying, permission from CANCOPY (Canadian Copyright Licensing Agency), 1 Yonge Street, Suite 1900, Toronto, Ontario M5E 1E5.

Nimbus Publishing Limited
PO Box 9166, Halifax, NS   B3K 5M8
(902) 455-4286

Printed and bound in Canada

National Library of Canada Cataloguing in Publication Data
    Creighton, Norman
        Talk about the valley: stories from Nova Scotia's Annapolis Valley
        Includes index.
        ISBN 1-55109-377-4
    1. Annapolis Valley (N.S.) I. Sircom, Hilary II. Title.

FC2345.A4C74 2001   971.6'33   C2001-902732-X
F1039.A2C74 2001

Canada   The Canada Council | Le Conseil des Arts
          for the Arts | du Canada

We acknowledge the financial support of the Government of Canada through the Book Publishing Industry Development Program (BPIDP) and the Canada Council for our publishing activities.

Photo/Illustration Credits

Annapolis Valley Historical Society, Middleton, NS: 47

Charles I. Bezanson, Lockhartville, NS: 167 (courtesy Hugh and Pam Nickerson, Port Williams, NS)

Bridgetown and Area Historical Society, Bridgetown, NS: 51, 171

A. B. Creighton, Scarborough, ON: 16, 18, 19, 20, 27, 30, 46, 61, 64, 65, 72, 76, 84, 87, 102, 117, 118, 121, 139, 175, 178 (details from paintings); 46, 85, 138 (oils); 141, 157, 183 (drawings); 2, 7, 9, 10, 13, 14, 15, 17, 31, 38, 41, 42, 50, 68, 69, 70, 74, 77, 78, 89, 94, 97, 105, 113, 120, 122, 126, 129, 131, 140, 142, 144, 155, 159, 160, 165, 184, 185 (watercolours)

Creighton Collection: 1, 3, 4, 11, 32, 88, 180, 181

Mary Davies, Toronto, ON: 107, 108 (courtesy Lyn Cook, Westport, ON)

Eldridge Memorial Library, Sandy Cove, NS: 114, 116

Jan Goodlad, Windsor, NS: 22, 23 (courtesy Hantsport Memorial Community Centre); 34 (courtesy Royal Bank, Windsor, NS); 37 (courtesy Don Davenport, Touchstone Pottery, Antigonish, NS); 92 (courtesy Carole Peterson, Falmouth, NS); 100, 127 (courtesy West Hants Historical Society); 136, 146, 147 (courtesy Olive Clark, Hantsport, NS); 137 (courtesy Sarah Mahoney, Windsor, NS); 145 (courtesy Marm's Barber Shop, Windsor, NS); 148 (courtesy Utopia, Windsor, NS); 150 (courtesy Phyllis Holmes, Hantsport, NS); 151, 173 (courtesy Eileen Withers, Windsor, NS); 152 (courtesy Sheri's Antiques, Hantsport, NS); 176 (courtesy Helen Hendry, Windsor, NS); 6, 39, 40, 57, 75, 81, 83, 98, 143, 153, 154, 162, 163, 169, 170 and all A. B. Creighton paintings

Hantsport Historical Society, Hantsport, NS: 149, 158, 180

Town of Hantsport: 21

Old Postcards: 172 (courtesy St. Clair Patterson, Hantsport, NS); 33, 36, 80, 179

Joseph Purcell, Lunenburg, NS: 25 (the original painting by Joseph Purcell of Lunenburg, Nova Scotia, Canada is part of the private collection of CKF Inc. and Minas Basin Pulp and Power Co., Ltd., Hantsport, NS)

Reid's Studio, Windsor, NS: 127 (courtesy West Hants Historical Society)

Cheryl Rutledge, Falmouth, NS: 166 (original watercolour)

Jenny Sheito, Port Williams, NS: 82 (oil copy of an unsigned painting of the Cornwallis area)

Jack Sheriff, Kipawo Showboat Company, Wolfville, NS: 43, 44, 45

Julie Sircom, Westcock, NB: 73 (courtesy Black Cultural Centre for NS, Westphal, NS)

Robert and Hilary Sircom, Hantsport, NS: 55 (courtesy Jim and Pauline How, Annapolis Royal, NS); 101 (courtesy Leon Fuller, Welsford, NS); 104 (courtesy Scott and Susan Ritchie, Bridgetown, NS); 123 (courtesy Linden and Mary Turnbull, Digby, NS); 13, 53, 54, 59, 60, 63, 90, 96, 99, 110, 111, 112, 133, 134, 156, 168

Acknowledgements

Heartfelt thanks to Jan Goodlad, administrator of the Norman Creighton estate, for the countless hours she has put into research, editing, and photography for this project. Her generous contribution of time and expertise has made this book possible.

For their encouragement and support, we thank Helen Hendry, Windsor; Heather Davidson and Bob Sircom, Hantsport; and Pat McLeod, Qualicum Beach, B.C.

Others whose assistance is gratefully acknowledged are Hansel Cook of Dalhousie University Archives; Beth Caldwell, Temporary Solutions, Hantsport; Sobeys Photo Lab, Windsor; and CBC Radio.

Part of the pleasure of compiling this book has been in finding pictures, in addition to those provided by Alan Creighton, to complement the text. We thank the many people who have assisted us in our search, particularly those connected with the Valley's museums and historical societies.

We also wish to thank all our friends who opened their homes to us and allowed us to photograph their treasures and memorabilia. Individual picture credits can be found on page ii.

Contents

Photo/Illustration Credits ii
Acknowledgements iii
Map of Nova Scotia and Annapolis Valley . . vi
Foreword 1
Introduction: Two Brothers 2
Poem: Artist on the Shore 6

Places 8

The Avon River 9
Poem: Blomidon Speaks 15
Fishing on the Avon 16
The Town That Once Built Ships 21
Autumn on the Half Shell 27
The Secret Prosperity of the
　Annapolis Valley 31
Some Maritime Mysteries in Stone 34
Wells 36
Swimming in Minas Basin 40
Poem: Flood Tide 42
Wolfville's International Festival 43

Wilmot Spa Springs 46
Bridgetown 50
A Visit to Annapolis Royal 53
Sandy Cove 57

People 62

Then and Now 63
Sidehill Farmers 66
Poem: Landscape 68
Grand Pré Revisited 69
William Hall—V.C. 73
The Truth About Men of Iron,
　Ships of Wood 76
Poem: Sea Morning 78
The Man From Noggin Corner 79
The Man With a Curse on His Field 82
Bucknam Pasha—A Boy From
　Halls Harbour 85
The Man Who Put Us on the Map 89
Charms of Boredom 92

Poem: Pastoral 94	Our Good Friend, the Horse 141
The Burgess Family 95	Poem: Stockyards 144
Windsor's Unsung Inventor 98	The Barber Shop 145
Alfred Fuller—And His Brush Company . .100	The Ice-box 147
A Visit With Ernest Buckler 104	That Brass Spittoon 149
The Magical Miss Mittens 107	The Grand-daddy Armchair 151
A Wartime Ghost Story 110	Royal Road to Reading 153
Poem: Coastal Spring 113	The Thumbtack Gazette 156
Fountain of Youth 114	Belcher's Almanac 162
Mi'kmaq Medicines 117	Poem: Fences 165
Poem: Whose Lake? 120	Fireplaces—And What They Tell Us 166
Pioneer Pollution Fighter 121	The Front Door Key—And Security 169
The Bird Woman of Nova Scotia 123	Old Postcards 170
The Lightning Slingers 125	Hazards of Larceny 173
	The Cord Saver .175
WAY OF LIFE 130	Patches 177
Sabbath Observance 131	Every Night at Seven 180
The Family Pew .133	Postscript 185
The Family Bible 136	Index of Nova Scotia Place Names 186
Joys of Travelling by Rail 138	

The Annapolis Valley

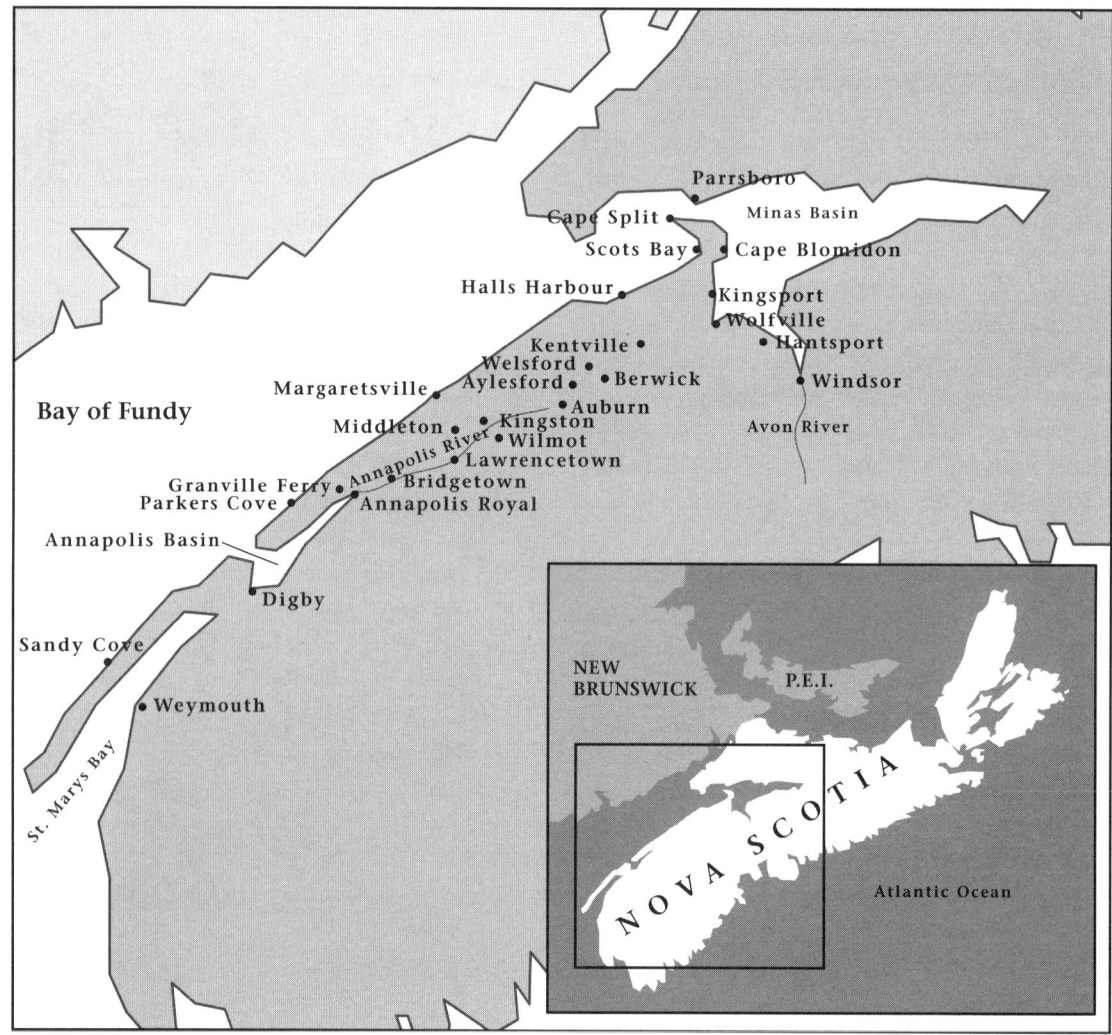

Foreword

Talk About the Valley is the second book of essays, originally written for broadcasting, by freelance writer and broadcaster, Norman Creighton. During the 1960s and 70s his friendly voice was familiar to Maritimers as he gave more than 600 talks which were aired on CBC's "A.M. Chronicle," "Maritime Magazine," and "Radio Noon."

The first book, Talk About the Maritimes, as its title suggests, is concerned with a wider area, while this book concentrates on the Annapolis Valley region of Nova Scotia. The essays are about places in the Valley, the people who have lived here and their way of life.

We are fortunate that Norman's older brother, Alan, in addition to being a poet and writer, is an accomplished artist. Some of his charming watercolour sketches of Valley scenes are reproduced here for the first time. Naturally, in black and white they lose much of the original artistry, however, they add immensely to the authenticity and flavour of the book. We thank Alan for his generosity in allowing them to be used. We are also grateful for permission to use some of the poems from Alan's collection, which were published as *Earth Call*, in 1936, and *Cross-Country*, in 1939.

Norman Creighton, circa 1950.

Alan Creighton, 1936.

Introduction
Two Brothers

Alan (born 1903) and Norman Creighton (1909-1995) were the sons of Charles and Harriet (Hendry) Creighton. An older son died as a child and there were two older sisters, Laleah and Marjorie. The early years of their lives were spent in Bedford, NS.

In 1932, the Creightons bought a house on Hantsport's Avon Street. Here they spent their summers until 1937 when, on Charles Creighton's retirement, it became their permanent home. The family soon made friends with their neighbours, settled into the daily patterns of the community, and enjoyed the leisurely pace of life in rural Nova Scotia.

The Creighton property was on both sides of Avon Street. At the back of the house a long garden ran down to Willow Brook. The garden was a constant source of joy and wonder to Norm. As a young man he had tuberculosis, and periods of ill health followed in later life. At these times he found solace and rejuvenation in country pursuits. He was a great believer in organic gardening and the holistic approach to health. The family enjoyed the

"...the Creightons bought a house on Hantsport's Avon Street."

fresh vegetables, fruit, honey, and mead, which Norm produced. He kept hens, and this photograph from the 30s shows Alan standing in front of the chicken house. This same chicken house was used by Norm as a writing retreat in the forties and fifties, and later by Alan as a studio. It was heated by the old brooder stove.

Across the road from the house, a field of lupins leads to the bank of the Avon River. Opposite, across the water and the red mud flats of low tide, is the Summerville Shore. Away in the distance to the north are Minas Basin and the dramatic silhouette of Cape Blomidon. Norm often wrote about this view from the riverbank and Alan sketched the scene many times over the years.

◆

Alan has been artist, musician, and writer. While living in Halifax, he attended the Victoria School of Art and Design, as a student of Elizabeth Nutt. He also studied violin under Ifan Williams at the Halifax Conservatory of Music. Alan might have continued with his artistic career, but with the need to earn a living, he went to business college and, for a while, became a reporter for the *Halifax*

Alan standing in front of the chicken house.

Chronicle covering court cases and shipping news.

After a short period in the States, Alan returned to Halifax to study piano. For several years he played the piano in movie theatres to accompany the silent films of that era. At the same time, he was contributing poems and short stories to American and Canadian magazines, including *Canadian Forum* and *Saturday Night*. In 1936, Alan's first book of poetry was published and the next year he moved to Toronto and worked with Hilda Ridley, preparing an anthology of Canadian poetry. Alan's work was well received and led to other opportunities.

In 1941, he joined the staff of *Canadian Forum* and worked there for 14 years. He was assistant editor during the time that Northrop Frye was editor. In 1956, Alan teamed up with Lou Morris, who had been the business manager at *Canadian Forum*, to open Old Favourites Antiquarian Bookstore in Toronto. Here they found they could make a better living than in the magazine business and Alan stayed with the bookstore until his retirement in 1978.

Throughout his years at the bookstore, Alan continued to paint. Some of his paintings, displayed on the store's walls, were sold. Summer holidays in Hantsport provided an opportunity to concentrate on his sketches and watercolours. He was a familiar figure in his white sun-hat with his sketchbook and folding stool.

On his retirement from bookselling, Alan moved from Rosedale to Scarborough, Ontario, where he still lives.

◆

Six years younger than Alan, Norm always admired his older brother and looked to him for advice as he also made writing his career. Many letters flowed between the brothers and Norm took a writing course by correspondence. He had articles accepted by several magazines and by the Canadian Broadcasting Company. In 1941, he was asked to become the scriptwriter for a new CBC farm family serial, "The Gillans," modelled on a programme already started in Ontario.

"The Gillans" was first broadcast in January 1942 and quickly became a Maritime institution. For seven and a half years, Norm wrote five scripts a week which he sent into Halifax on the train so that the actors could read their parts "live" on air each weekday.

The two brothers at the Hantsport house, circa 1935.

Writing the script was demanding enough, but what was even more time consuming was the endless research required. Since the broadcasts were heard throughout the Maritimes, a location for the Gillans' farm was never specifically stated, but Norm obviously drew on his experience of country life in his part of the Annapolis Valley. He relied on neighbours and local farmers to fill in details of farm practices and traditions, and was frequently in touch with experts at the Experimental Farm in Kentville.

Norm was amazed by the fan mail he received. When the pressure of the daily deadline eventually became too much and he had to pass his job on to successor Kay Hill, he was overwhelmed by the outpouring of affection and concern from his listeners. To many people, the Gillans had become as much a part of the family as their actual relatives.

Norm continued his writing career with articles and stories appearing in *Maclean's, Saturday Night* and *Weekend Magazine,* but he felt he needed more writing experience and training. From 1955 to 1962 he lived in the

U.S. and Mexico. He worked and studied in New York with a view to writing for the new medium of television and with the hope of breaking into the fiction market. Ultimately, he was to find his strength lay in documentary writing.

In 1966, Norm returned to Hantsport and became a freelance writer and broadcaster. His experience with "The Gillans" had earned him many friends and contacts; he had a most inquiring mind and made it his business to find out the facts on an amazing number of topics. He was an inveterate letter writer and sent away for numerous pamphlets and magazines, which could add to his knowledge of places, events and country pursuits. Thus, he gathered material for the talks, which made his name a household word.

By this time technology had made some advances and, instead of sending scripts into Halifax, Norm soundproofed a room in the house to function as his recording studio. Here he was able to record his own voice on a reel-to-reel tape recorder. However, he still had to meet his deadline by sending the tapes into Halifax on the train.

Nothing can take the place of Norm's distinctive radio voice and his calm deliberate delivery. Perhaps, however, the printed word may allow the reader time to linger over the historical oddities he hunted out and to appreciate the gentle humour that characterized his talks.

In their words and pictures the Creighton brothers have provided us with a tapestry of Annapolis Valley life in times gone by. This is a part of our heritage and we hope that the book will find its way into schools and libraries so that succeeding generations may have some idea of the way we were. For this reason it is dedicated to the young people of the Annapolis Valley.

H.J.S. 2001

NOTE

Square brackets indicate editor's notes. They are generally found at the ends of the pieces. Dates have been inserted where it helps the reader to have this detail, but many of the original manuscripts cannot be dated accurately.

There are a few words found here which may not be familiar to today's readers. For example, barn *linters* does not appear in any modern dictionary, and *farewell summer* is a flower name that is not now commonly used. These and other curiosities add to the charm of the pieces, which have been edited as lightly as possible.

As Norm rarely divulged his sources, and as most of the books and magazines he used as reference material have been dispersed, we must beg the reader's indulgence for any errors in the facts presented here.

Artist on the Shore

No colour anywhere today!
A wide gloom fills
The leaden spaces across the bay
Between dead hills.

The heavy shore is dull and old
And grayly known;
The lurching waves come bare and cold
To fall alone ...
◆
(And then you come in your faded dress...)
Whole continents die;
New vibrant purple hills caress
A silver sky;

And fresh-toned music ripples free—
Along the shore;
With living hues upon the sea
Not there before!

Alan Creighton

PLACES

Places

If the town of Windsor considers itself to be "The Gateway to the Annapolis Valley" in the east, then Digby should be considered the entry point in the west. However, for the purpose of this book, a somewhat broader area has been included. For example, there are pieces here which are concerned with Falmouth, near Windsor, and with Sandy Cove, which is 12 miles from Digby on Digby Neck.

The map shows the Valley proper to be that part of the province which runs parallel to the Bay of Fundy and which is drained by the Annapolis River. The river has its source in the Caribou Bog near Aylesford and flows out into the Annapolis Basin at Annapolis Royal. It is bordered on one side by the North Mountain and on the other by the Southern Uplands. At its eastern end, Wolfville Ridge slopes southward to the Gaspereau River, which flows into Minas Basin near Grand Pré. This area is dominated by the distant prospect of Cape Blomidon.

Strung along the floor of the Valley, on the old Number One Highway, are the small towns which visitors find similar to the towns of New England with their tree-lined main streets, dignified old churches and elegant homes. On the slopes of the North and South Mountains are the small holdings referred to by Norm as sidehill farms. The Valley is an agricultural area famous for its apple orchards. In springtime crowds of visitors come to be photographed among the blossoms. In the fall they return for apples and other fruits and vegetables.

Any part of the Valley can be reached on a day trip by car from Hantsport. Via Rail also used to run a regular service down the Valley and Norm enjoyed travelling by train. If no transportation was available, then Norm got what information he needed by mail. He carried on a voluminous correspondence with many friends.

What we have here is one man's view of the place he knew best and for which he had a great affection. One might think he would see the Valley through rose-coloured spectacles, but this was not the case; he saw it with all its wrinkles.

The Avon River

My home is on the bank of a river, a very lovely river, called the Avon. Now, there's a river in England with the same name but they say it differently; over there they say "A-v'n." In Hantsport, we call it the Avon, and we consider it a very fine part of the landscape. It is a river full of variety—of movement and constant change; in fact, so much change that people from outside find it disconcerting. Most of them seem to prefer a river which runs in one direction all the time. The Avon finds this too monotonous; twice a day, with the turn of the tide, it starts running in the opposite direction. I've lived beside a tidal river now so long, I don't know if I could get used to an ordinary river that runs only the one way. For one thing there'd be nothing to talk about.

Take our river now—it's a never-failing topic of conversation. Is the tide in or is the tide out? You see, it makes a great difference. If the tide is in, then you can go swimming, or sailing, or fishing. But if the tide is out—well, then you can go for a walk out into the middle of the riverbed, look for amethysts, or pick up pieces of rock that might be fossils.

There are so many things to be seen in the Avon River. Yet, outsiders who come here are often critical of it, simply because it's a river with character and a mind of its own. Here is what one visitor, a Mr. Noble, said in the nineteenth century: *The Avon River would have been a charming river—if there had been a drop of water in it.* These tourists always arrive at low tide. He goes on: *I never knew how much water adds to a river. Its slimy bottom was quite a ghast-*

"My home is on the bank of a river, a very lovely river..."

ly spectacle, an ugly rent in the land that nothing could heal but the friendly returning tide. I should think it would be confusing, to dwell by a river that runs first one way, and then the other—and then vanishes altogether.

It isn't, really. You get used to it. As I say, it gives us all so much to talk about. In the wintertime, our river never freezes up—it doesn't get a chance to. It just forms great ice cakes that drift back and forth with the tides. You can hear them on a still morning, crushing and grinding against each other. As the winter wears on, these junks of ice keep rolling over in the water, growing bigger all the time, till some of them are like baby icebergs as high as a house. Some of these icebergs we come to recognize; they develop a personality. Perhaps one of them is frozen to a piece of pulpwood, or another has picked up a big stone in its journeys up and down the river. Some take on peculiar shapes. You look out the window at breakfast time and exclaim, "Oh, there goes that big ice cake again—the one with the seagull roosting on top. Isn't it a monster? It will be a long time before he disappears." Then, when March comes along, we watch the big ice-cake shrink and melt away, a little each day; we know spring is coming. So our river is a kind of almanac, helping us to keep track of the year. It is a barometer too! All you have to do is stand on the bank and listen. If you can hear the voices of men talking in Summerville, on the other side of the river, it means that we're going to have fine weather—or rain. I'm

"I never saw so much mud!"

not sure which. You see, it shows the air is very clear and carrying, and that means something, but I forget just what.

Outsiders don't realize how useful the Avon River is. They are always criticizing it because the water is not crystal clear, the way it is on the South Shore. Then, when the tide goes out and they don't have to look at the water any more, they start finding fault with the mud. One of them turned to me and said, in a voice touched with awe, "I never saw so much mud!" They would not dream of going bathing in our river. Oh dear no, the water's too muddy. It is no use to tell them it's all an optical illusion—that the water is really clear. They will not believe you. I am not saying the water isn't a *little* muddy—but it's good clean mud. As kids we always felt the mud was one of the main attractions of summer bathing. One of our most popular summer sports was mudbank-sliding. You find a high steep mudbank, and then you slide down into the river, or what's left of it. Sometimes we used a sort of toboggan on the slippery slope of a mudbank; you developed quite an exhilarating speed before you hit the water. Not just the kids enjoy the mud; it is highly esteemed by the dogs of Hantsport, who love to race up and down the beach, chasing seagulls and sand-peeps and getting their fur thoroughly coated with mud. Then, tired but happy, their legs wet and dripping, they trot home and settle themselves down on the best chesterfield while the lady of the house busies herself with the mop and vacuum cleaner.

I'm giving you the impression that the Avon is a muddy river and that is not so. Above the tidewater, above the Sangster Bridge, the water is as clear and sparkling as any trout stream you ever waded in. It continues for miles, away back in the Southern Uplands, out past Three Lakes, and Vaughan and Long Lake. Here it is used to develop hydro power. Sometimes the people of Halifax run short of electricity and buy some of this power from

"...mud was one of the main attractions of summer bathing."

Avon River hydro plants; so you see, the Avon is helping to keep the lights on in Halifax.

In the early days, before hydro power was ever thought of, these headwaters of the Avon were the source of great timber wealth. One company had a sluice eleven miles long. Lumber, mostly deal, was sluiced down this to the loading docks at Windsor Forks. Here it was piled onto scows, and towed downstream to where the ship was waiting—generally off Horton Bluff. The ships were mostly square-riggers in those days, anywhere from fifteen hundred to two thousand tons, and they would carry about a million feet of lumber. It took them a month to get loaded. The crew, however, had a quicker method. In the evenings they came ashore at Avonport and made for the Oakland Inn. This was an old coach inn, and like all inns in those days they served wine and spirits. The crew generally managed to get loaded in considerably less than a month! Incidentally, the old Oakland Inn is still there, but now [1950] it is a general store and gas station. In those unrepentant days, the wharf at Avonport would often echo to the songs of a roistering band of sailor men making their way back to the lumber ship anchored off the Bluff.

The other day I was chatting with a neighbour of mine who went to sea on one of the old square-riggers. He gave me a few facts about the life and you may find them of interest. Members of the crew signed on for three years: that is, you received no pay until the end of three years (except a small advance when you went ashore at a foreign port). The pay: Captain, $80 a month; Mate, $45 a month; Second Mate, $25; Able Seaman, $15 a month. That was the traditional pay for Able Seamen out of English ports—three pounds ten a month. As to food—corned beef, potatoes, boiled rice, corn meal mush, salt pork, and hard tack. But there were compensations. In Jamaica, the seamen could buy a basket of fruit—one of those flat baskets the women carry on their heads, holding almost a bushel of fruit, such as bananas, oranges, tangerines, pimentos, a few pineapples—the whole thing for 25 cents. Rum was 20 cents a bottle, so a sailor didn't need too many cents to paint the town red.

Today, lumber is still shipped from Avon River ports. And, as in the old days, it goes almost entirely to the export market—to the United Kingdom, the Continent, South America. But the tonnage is small compared with another Avon River export—gypsum.

You can see the white gypsum cliffs at a dozen points all the way up the river. Quarrying of gypsum began a hundred years ago and maybe more. I was talking recently with a man who can remember when the quarrying was done without machinery. The rock was broken up into lumps big enough for a man to handle. Then it was hauled out of the quarry by a horse-drawn cart and dumped onto the wharf. Here, men with wheelbarrows wheeled it onto the ship and stowed it away

"...the white gypsum cliffs..."

in the hold. It took two tides (and sometimes three) to load a vessel of four hundred tons. Today, by means of a conveyor belt, they load a steamer of ten *thousand* tons inside of two hours. The men with wheelbarrows would have needed about three months to do the job.

In terms of tonnage, the Avon is an important waterway, and this is not a new thing. In the days of wooden ships, the shores along the Avon rang to the music of broadaxe and adze; shipbuilding was in its heyday. At one time, Hantsport was listed fifth among the world's shipbuilding centres. We hear much of the importance of Canada's export trade. Avon River ports have been contributing to this export trade for generations.

Somehow, the commercial aspects of the Avon seem insignificant when one views the timeless scene of the river with its backdrop of wooded hills. For countless days and nights these waters have flooded in over Crowell's Bar, and felt their way up the inner reaches of her tributaries, the Kennetcook and Cogmagun Rivers.

You sit here on the bank watching the current swirling out past Blue Beach and the sight of that ebbing water drains anxiety from the mind. You forget about the cost-of-living index and the life insurance premium that's overdue...for it's late in the evening, and the seagulls are flying down from Windsor, on their way home for the night, to their nesting grounds on Boot Island. A dog is barking across the river and it is hard to believe he's

"...by means of a conveyor belt, they load...inside of two hours."

two miles away. Summerville seems so close to us, with its white steepled church, and its Lombardy poplars, its graveyard, and its twisting road, starting at the wharf and winding up over the hill.

As the sky darkens over Minas Basin, we look out across fifteen miles of water to the towering heights of Cape Blomidon, silhouetted against the night sky—rising five hundred feet above the beach. This is the home of Glooscap, Great Spirit of the Mi'kmaq. Already the lighthouses are blinking at Kingsport, and Parrsboro, and Horton Bluff, also the lights of the gas fairway buoys, marking the channel. There is another light, off the tail of the Western Bar. That is a gypsum boat. It must be the *Gypsum Queen*, which is due from Philadelphia. She won't be docking until one or two in the morning. Customs Inspector, Walter Comstock, will be up pretty late tonight.

Out on the river you can hear voices. The drifters have started drifting their nets for gaspereau. They are the men from Card Beach and Michener Point and Upper Falmouth, shouting back and forth, exchanging talk from one boat to another. The little red lights on their flag-buoys, on the ends of their nets, show through the darkness, bobbing along on the fast-moving tide like sea-going will-o'-the-wisps. Yes, it's not a bad river, the Avon River...in spite of all that mud.

"Summerville...with its white steepled church..."

BLOMIDON SPEAKS

From hot Triassic days,
The pulse of boiling seas,
Heavily remote,
I have watched your coming
Across the ages.
Now I laugh at your orchards,
The bloom of your pale valleys.
Against the far knowledge of my blue slope
Your years and doings
Are as a scattering of wild roses
Or the tinkle of a cow-bell
On the summer wind.

Alan Creighton

Fishing on the Avon

He was fifteen feet long, weighed over a ton, and the trouble was he wouldn't get away. He just lay there on the beach and we did not know what to do with him. He was what they call a black fish.

Perhaps it is stretching the point a little to say I caught him. He just drifted in on our beach and when the tide went out there he was, stranded on the sand. We all crowded down onto the beach, took pictures of him, and assured each other that he might be worth a lot of money—if you could find some use for him. No one seemed to have any suggestions, so finally a motorboat came and, at high tide, everyone pushed and shoved until the black fish was set adrift. Then they towed him out into Minas Basin. That was my first fish; from now on they get smaller.

But just a word more about these black fish. They are really not fish at all but a species of whale. The incident I speak of took place around 1932. That summer a whole school of them came up the Avon River as far as Hantsport. The people watched uneasily as the big fish rolled and sported on the incoming tide. For the black fish had entered the Avon

"...the black fish were carted off for fertilizer."

once before, in 1885, and at that time their coming had spelled affliction for almost every one of the town's three hundred homes.

A few days ago, I was talking with one of our town's oldest and most respected citizens, Mr. James Borden, who can remember those days. He gave me some of the background of the tragedy.

The fish were strangers in these waters; no one in the town had ever seen a black fish before, and they did not realize the danger they ran in killing them. One can picture the excitement when these giant creatures were sighted out in midstream, moving swiftly past Hantsport upstream towards Windsor. Whales! Sperm oil! There were those who had cousins or friends in New England, who had written of the whaling fleet, of the fabulous wealth of New Bedford and Nantucket—and here it was being swept in on the tide to our very doorstep. Before any plan of action could be hit upon, the tide had turned and the black fish were soon beached, stranded out on the sandbars. It was easy enough to kill them. Some were skinned for the oil, but it was more of a job than the town had bargained for. The nearby farmers took a hand and the black fish were carted off for fertilizer. Mr. Borden can remember seeing an ox-drawn cart, with the head of the big fish lying on the tongue between the two oxen, and its tail dragging on the ground behind. It was 25 feet long. The farmers tried to compost them, but they did not bury the fish deeply enough. Soon a strange fever broke out; they called it the black fish cholera. Thirty people lost their lives. So when the black fish returned again in the thirties, it's no wonder they towed them out to sea.

Another story of a school of fish that came to these waters has a happier

"...the Gaspereau River."

ending. It was at the mouth of the Gaspereau River, at Horton, in the year 1898. Someone had put out a seine that year, to catch shad. Fortune favoured him. On the very first day, he caught a barrel of shad, and the season was only just beginning. As the days went by, the shad were more and more plentiful. With each new tide, the seine was alive with them. There was no let-up; every day it got better—his net was positively bursting with shad. He would no sooner get rid of one catch than he would have another on his hands, and bigger than the last.

One morning when this fortunate fisherman went down to the shore to check his seine, he could not believe his eyes. The bunt of his seine, a circle 75 feet across, was two feet deep in shad. They were beauties—all of them, shimmering in the morning sun, fresh out of the water. What in the world could he do with them? Everyone from Hard Scrabble Mountain to Kentville had been eating shad for weeks. They had had them baked, boiled and fried, done in vinegar, spiced with cloves. By its very abundance this good fish had worn its welcome thin. There was just no one left who wanted a fresh shad, and here were thousands of them. It would take him all his days to salt them all himself. He flinched at the prospect. He'd had enough of shad for one season. So what did he do? He sent word out that anyone who wanted could come down to the seine and help himself. With that, wagons started streaming across Grand Pré dykes, from Hortonville, Avonport, and the Gaspereau Valley. They tell me that, in that year, everyone within a radius of five miles had a barrel of salt shad tucked away in the cellar. I can't imagine anything nicer.

In those days you could buy a shad for ten cents. As for gaspereau, a neighbour of mine tells me of fishing for gaspereau when he was a young lad and all he got was a cent a piece, a dollar a hundred. Of course, at the beginning of the season, when they were still a novelty, you might peddle a few of them at 30 cents a dozen. Pretty soon they would drop to 20 cents a dozen…15 cents….But when you bought them in quantity, for salting down, the price was a dollar a hundred.

Here I am reminiscing about old times as if there were no fish left in the Avon—and there certainly are! If you want proof of that, step out here on the riverbank, any time from now until the middle of August, and you will see a little fleet of boats moving quietly along

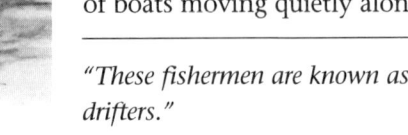

"These fishermen are known as drifters."

with the current. Off from the stern of each boat a ways, there is a flag-buoy marking the end of the net.

These fishermen are known as drifters. They seldom use the motors in their boats; they just drift along, allowing the ebb and flow of the tide to carry them out to the black buoy where they pull their nets. Then, as the tide returns, they pay out their nets and drift back upstream to their homes at Card Beach, Mount Denson, and Falmouth, where they dispose of their catch. These men live on their boats. They are on the river day and night, following the tides. At night you will see red lights glowing from their flag-buoys. These tell them how their nets lie and are a warning to shipping. As far as I know there has never been an accident at night on the Avon. The drifters are on the river five days a week. On Friday evening they all come home for the weekend, for there is a law which forbids anyone from drifting from Friday at sundown to the nearest tide at Monday morning's sunrise. Over the weekend the fish have the river all to themselves, but, with the first tide on Monday, the men are out on the stream again paying out their nets.

"...they all come home for the weekend..."

Viewed from the shore, drifting looks like a peaceful occupation, and on sunny days it must be pleasant indeed, swinging along on the tide, while you sit there smoking your pipe and watching the bobs to see if the fish are hitting. But every day is not a sunny day, and they tell me that pulling in the nets can be hard, backbreaking work. These men are real full-time fishermen during the months when the gaspereau and shad are running.

One summer, my brother and I decided we would make a great saving in the grocery bill by catching our own fish. The fish were out there—free for the taking. All you had to do was catch them. How would we go about it? One of our neighbours told us of a very ingenious contraption, popular in Bay of Fundy waters, and known as a weir. It is a sort of wire fence, so shaped that it forms a trap that catches the bewildered fish, leaving them stranded, high and dry when the tide goes down. It sounded like a capital plan. Once the weir was constructed there would be no more work. We would simply stroll down the beach after each tide, pick off the fish and pop them into a basket. All right then, we would build a weir.

Like so many simple ideas, it proved to be surprisingly complex.

The site we had chosen was halfway down the beach and would be well covered at high tide. We started inshore with the small end of the wing of the weir. As we extended the wing down the beach, it grew higher and the beach grew muddier. Struggling to keep the taller poles upright, we found ourselves sinking deeper and deeper into the mud. We soon realized that lumberman's rubber boots were not suitable footwear for this type of work. They sank down into the mud so far that when you tried to free your foot, it came away minus the boot. There you were, balancing on one leg, with the other stockinged foot in the air, trying to wrench your boot from the mud. So we invested in two pairs of hip rubber boots which did not come off so easily. Of course they cost us about ten dollars. Then, by the time we reached the end of the wing and got started on the barb, our weir had risen to staggering heights and we had to send to the store for two more rolls of chicken wire. However, we felt we would get our money back when we started catching fish.

We finally got the weir finished. Then we sat back and waited. Nothing happened. The tides came and went, and left our weir with nothing but seaweed…or an occasional eel…or a brown-backed flounder. Then, one day, we went to the edge of the bank and looked down on the beach, and there, lying in the barb of the weir, on the brown mud were half a dozen beautiful white fish.

We called a neighbour to come and share our triumph. He said, "Why, you've caught some bass."

Well, we knew it had been worth waiting for! Bass—fresh from our own weir! We hurried down the ladder onto the beach carrying baskets, but my excitement was so great that, when I bent over to pick up the bass I lost my balance and, in trying to regain it, I fell back into the mud.

There was not much profit on those bass, but I'll say this: they were the sweetest tasting fish I ever ate. We stuffed them and baked them in the oven, and we all agreed that, after all, there's nothing like fish out of your own weir.

The Town That Once Built Ships

Where I live, in Hantsport, Nova Scotia, they use the same language I'm using now. But there was a time when they didn't. There was a time when they talked another language—when they used words like dubber, fid, trunnel, cringe-ring, stanchions, bile brace, carlin beams, and pintles. That is the lingo of shipbuilding.

The seal of the town of Hantsport bears the picture of a sailing ship. Yet I doubt if there's one man on the Town Council who can name the rigging on that ship. Fifty years ago, almost every lad in the village could tell you the difference between a forelower tops'l yard and a t'gallant yard and a royal. Boys love to play around ships, and down at the wharf there was always a barque or brigantine in from Cardiff or Bremerhaven or Trinidad. At the shipyards, you could watch the broadaxman hewing out timbers. You could hunt for old copper nails in among the chips, and if you got a pound of them, they'd pay you four cents. The boss of a planking gang might even notice you long enough to give you a piece of pitch to chew. Talk about fun! Why wouldn't a boy know all about lining a plank and spinning oakum by the time he was out of short pants? When you lived in a town that had but one single passion—to build ships and sail them—you had to know these things. Even the womenfolk knew that to "pay the decks" you needed no money—just a potful of boiling pitch to pour into the deck seams. When a man said to you, "How many knees can you fay in a day?" you didn't think he was slightly fey himself. You knew he was a ship's carpenter, and he was asking you how fast you could work at fitting knees into place in a ship's hull.

But today, the people in Hantsport could not tell you the difference between a dubber and a beetler. A rudder pintle means no more to them than a butt spike. They just don't know. And to think, this was the town that once ranked fifth place among the ship-building centres of the world. Now they could not step and rig a lowermast to save their souls. What happened? Why, iron ships came in and took the place of wooden ships. It does not matter how well you build a ship, if there's no market for it.

For years now, in talking with the older folks in my home town, I've detected a note of sadness, of homesickness for those earlier days when the whole town was bound together by the call of the sea. That was up to about the turn of the century, and then, suddenly, it all came to an end. The town was left like a tree

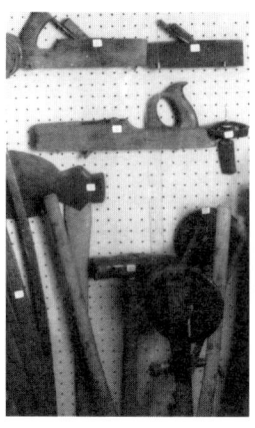

Shipbuilding tools displayed in Churchill House Marine Room, Hantsport.

with the tap-root cut away. As the years went on, new industries sprang up to replace the shipyards, but they were not the same; those who could remember the smell of boiling tar and the ring of a corking mallet became exiles in a strange country, a country that talked of pulpwood and paper pie plates—excellent things, but somehow not very exciting.

I tried to reconstruct the town as it had been in the late nineties; my attempts to sketch out a picture met with failure. There was so little left to go on. Almost every trace of the shipyards has been obliterated. One of them is grown up in alder bushes and grey birch. All I could find was a rotting bed-log and, on the sandy beach, the tide had uncovered some deck spikes and a cringle-ring. Yet, during the nineteenth century, one yard alone had turned out 99 ships—most of them 'tweendeckers, from a thousand or two thousand tons—and those ships made a name for themselves from London to Singapore. There must be some evidence left, so, I began talking to people, asking them questions.

Those under forty remembered nothing, except hearsay. Their lives and interests centre largely in the manufacture of pulpwood. Two or three of the boys still ship out of here on gypsum boats but this is no longer the port that once produced 250 deep sea master mariners. That town belongs to the older generation.

I went to them and gradually, piece by piece, found what I was looking for. In one home would be a ship's model; in another, an oil-painting hung on the wall showing a barquentine under full sail entering Amsterdam. In those days it was the fashion to have your ship painted by a European artist while you were in port at Hamburg or Antwerp. Another large and beautiful oil painting depicted a Hantsport ship entering the harbour at Naples. Chinese artists painted some of the other ships—those in the China trade. Then there

"In one home would be a ship's model..."
Model of the brigantine Venture *made by Captain William Folker, Hantsport.*

"…it was the fashion to have your ship painted…"
Picture of Barque *Hamburg* built by Churchill Yard in 1886.

were the souvenirs: music boxes from Germany; shells from the Windward Islands; a piece of black coral from St. Kits; tortoise-shell baskets from Jamaica; water jars from the East Indies. These water jars were used to keep the drinking water cool on the long voyage back from the East. A rope was tied around its neck and it hung from a beam in the ceiling of the cabin, at a convenient height for drinking; they were made of porous clay which cooled the water by evaporation. Many of the souvenirs were birds—magpies, cockatoos, parrots. Only one parrot still survives, at the age of 45. There were ostrich eggs, from Africa. These were blown out, and a ribbon threaded through the two holes, and then it was hung on the what-not. The what-nots in Hantsport in those days were loaded to capacity.

At one home I was shown how the house was framed after the nature of a ship, with ship's knees instead of floor joists. The man who built this was a ship's carpenter and knew no other type of construction. It was braced and stayed as if to weather a tropical hurricane, and today that house stands as plumb and level as the day it was built.

Finally, I got in touch with two men who had worked in the shipyards. What I am telling you now is what they told me. When they started talking about shipbuilding, their eyes lighted up with the gladness of an artist contemplating his completed canvas. As they talked, Hantsport became peopled with another race of men—liners and bevelers, plankers and broadax-men, dubbers and auger men, hole borers, trunnel drivers, iron fasteners, riggers, sailmakers, and blockmakers. Last but not least was the ship's blacksmith, the man who banded the spars, welded anchor stocks, made chain plates for the rigging, trusses for the lower yards, and bands for the yards to slide up and down on.

They tell a story of one of those blacksmiths. The master shipbuilder came to him with the specifications for a new ship, and asked him to order the material for the necessary ironwork. The blacksmith made his estimate, and the material was ordered. After it came, he hammered out every piece of ironwork to the last eye bolt, and when he was through, he didn't have enough iron left to make an extra spar band. He had ordered neither too much nor too little, but just enough.

As these shipbuilders talked on, I saw the town in wintertime when, for a few months, the yards were idle while the men were out in the woods cutting the timbers for next year's ships. Some would spend the winter at the block factory making blocks and belaying pins; others worked making moulds for the frame of the ship they were going to build.

Spring sees the laying of a new keel; and from then on every man has his job. The riggers are off by themselves in a field cutting the rigging, putting eyes in it, splicing it. The broadax-men hew out the deck beams and stanchions. That was before the day of the bandsaw when all timber had to be hewn. Before long the planking gang moves in, and from then on it's a race. The caulkers vie with each other in threading oakum into the seams. One of these caulkers was ambidextrous and he always got ahead of everyone else, because when the others reached the end of their seam they had to walk back to the bow to tackle a new seam. He would shift over to his left hand and start working in the opposite direction. Of course you would not admit you were racing—you did not say to the other fellow, "I'm going to lay more plank than you." But uptown that evening you would hear someone say, "Well, we got on half a streak more than they did." Or you might hear a ship's carpenter say, "I fayed twelve knees today; he only got nine in." From the time they went to work until they knocked off, it was a contest. If two men were hewing a stick, they raced to get to the end, because the man who reached the end first had a little rest.

What did these men do for entertainment in the evenings. They would hang around the general store and talk about shipbuilding. There was no movie, no radio. Their one big interest was the ship. Listen to them talking:

"How much deck did they lay today?"

"That Buffalo rail doesn't look right to me—too much cant... "

"When do you suppose she'll be done?"

"Say, he's a greenhorn: doesn't know enough to dip his auger in fish-oil to make the chips come up the barrel. Reminds me, I forgot to pick up an armful of chips when I started for home tonight; won't have anything to light the fire with in the morning."

"They say Jud is quitting as boss rigger, bought himself a farm. Think he'll make a fetch of it?"

"Some of the boys are leaving for Bath, Maine; big shipyards down there... "

"Listen, I drove more trunnels than he did and I drove them in all the way too."

"Wonder if Ted'll have those deadeyes ready by tomorrow... "

"What you gonna do this fall, Al, after you finish rigging her?"

"Oh, guess I'll join the crew, jump aboard and go down south for the winter, be back in time to start work next spring."

And so they would chat and exchange sea yarns and watch this dream of theirs take shape day by day, till finally it came time to bend the sails. When she was finished, it was something they had made with their own hands. All of it. They followed her voyages about the world, looked for her name in the paper, made inquiries about her. She was their ship.

One of these men told me how as a boy he loved to stand and listen to the sounds of the shipyard. It was like a sort of music: some driving iron; some driving wooden trunnels; the broadax-men chopping away at the hatch combing; the adzemen swinging their adze with feather-edge precision as they dub the ship's bottom; the mallets of the ship's joiners; the mallets of the caulkers; hammers, pole-axes, everyone pounding for all he's worth. The noise was so great that at first it deafened you—you had to shout to talk to the man next to you. But to those who were part of it, it was harmony with its trebles and its basses, all in tune. The bassoon or tuba was a noble mallet known as the beetle, a big hardwood

"Launching day..."
Barque Forest, *Churchill shipyards, Hantsport, in 1873. Original oil painting by Joseph Purcell, of Lunenburg, NS.*

maul, wielded by a beetler who delivered his blows with a resounding clump. But soaring high above them all were the violins of this mighty orchestra—the caulking mallets. These were long thin mallets and the caulkers took great pride in making them ring. No caulker would use a dead mallet, they had to ring. They put a saw cut down through the middle to act as a sort of sounding board, and then the mallet rang like a bell. Cynics say it was to impress the boss with how hard they were working. I like to think they felt themselves part of a great symphony—a symphony that had as its finale…launching day.

Launching day—this meant excitement and fun! Just make for the shipyards. Where are the shipyards? Look up over the trees. See those four spars rising 140 feet in the air. The foreyard is 85 feet long and every inch of the rigging is decked out with coloured pennants and signal flags on the signal halyard. That is the *Evangeline*. She's due to be launched this afternoon at high tide. Follow the traffic! Already carriages and two-seated surreys from all over the country are streaming into the town.

The ladies of the Baptist church have a canteen right here at the shipyards, where they're serving tea and sandwiches. The girls are wearing their prettiest bonnets, because this is a holiday! They're launching a ship—a ship all of us…helped…to…build!

Autumn on the Half Shell

I thought this would be easy, but I was wrong. When they asked me to do these broadcasts, I said, "Sure, I'll do them; why not? I live in a small country town. The whole thing is right there in front of me. It's just a matter of talking about it, and you learned how to talk years ago, when you were a kid. This should be child's play." But that's where I made a mistake.

Of course, almost anyone can fill in fifteen minutes talking. I've known people to keep it up for hours, but it takes real staying power to be the person they're talking to. The patient radio listener is the real user of words—though what use he makes of all the words he hears I've never quite fathomed out.

It's autumn, and let's be honest—you don't want me going on about the trees turning colour, the pungent odour of burning leaves, the exhil-

"...the pungent odour of burning leaves..."

aration of the first frosty morning. You'll know all about that soon enough. Autumn is only autumn, when all is said and done. Such a lot of boring things can be said—and even done, at this time of year.

Those Michaelmas daisies, now, in the garden alongside our post office, why bother mentioning them? Their violet and lavender heads nod no more fetchingly in a small town than in a country hedgerow. Our street lights come on a few minutes earlier each evening, the way they do in Montreal and Toronto. And the way the sounds carry in this sparkling night air, so you can hear a dog barking all the way across on the other side of the Avon River....Well, I expect they kept you awake last night, too.

If only I could find some aspect of this autumn scene with a flavour all its own...so you will know that this is October in a little town, here in the Annapolis Valley, close to the pounding surf of the Bay of Fundy. What can you say about a small town, simply because it happens to be autumn? Our Board of Trade held it's first meeting of the season at the Town Hall last night…but that's going on all across the country. What if we are planting tulip bulbs and banking spruce boughs up around our rose bushes? Who cares? What you would like to hear about is something a bit different—wherein our town displays a certain individuality. As for instance, in the matter of taxis.

Toward late afternoon, when dusk creeps in over the salt marshes and the government wharf, our taxis light up a glass-covered sign on top of the car. That lets you know which taxi it is. Without this light we might mistake them for foreign taxis from a neighbouring town and forget to wave to them as they go hurtling up and down Main Street. There is something warm and reassuring about those taxis of ours, threading their way through the nighttime streets, with that cheerful glow held aloft like a jack-o'-lantern….Uh, what do you say? Your taxis have them too? Up on the roof? I can't talk about that, then.

Well, would you be interested in hearing that our town truck (the one with the right-hand drive, a leftover from the war) has been working at the gravel pit laying in a supply of sand for sanding the icy sidewalks next winter? No, I didn't think you would.

You probably also have a massed male choir who are starting to practise for the Christmas concert. I wish you could hear our choir sing "Dear Land of Home," by Sibelius….Your choir sings it too…? Oh….

So, what am I going to talk about? I gave my word I'd have something ready. I guess it's time I played my trump card—the hunger strike! So far it's never failed me. You just go without eating until your brain fetches up an idea.

Here, I must get busy. No thanks, I'm not having any breakfast. I think I'll go for a walk to see if I can't pick up some suggestions. Do you feel like coming along? Fine!

It's mild out this morning. It must have been a warm night. Folks are out after mushrooms. Do you see them over there on the dykes? It's only a step out of town, and our dykes are the greatest place for mushrooms—those little button mushrooms that look so attractive, creamed on toast. Some mornings you can gather a bushel basketful in no time. What do we do with so many? Put them down for winter in little hardwood kegs, with sliced nutmeg and distilled vinegar. They go so well with a steak, though down here in the Maritimes most of us can't afford to buy steak. I like them for breakfast, done with shredded parsley….But let's not talk about breakfast. How am I going to get this talk done? What on earth can you say about a small town in autumn? Our town is so small, only the one block, and we've already been around it twice. I don't see anything worth talking about….

Let's step into this grocery store, on the corner. It might give us an idea. I see they have a barrel of sauerkraut in. It's just been opened. Would you care for a taste? I don't think anyone's looking. I would like you to try it, because it is the best made in Canada....Where does it come from? Why, Lunenburg, of course. They've been making sauerkraut down in Lunenburg for almost two hundred years. You can't beat people who have had that much practice, and the cabbages they grow down there on the South Shore....Those cabbages are nourished by the fogs drifting in from Mahone Bay. It gives them a sea-born tang, so that after they've been fermented in vinegar, the sauerkraut has the very flavour of the Maritimes.

But here, what am I doing? I'm not allowed to eat anything until this talk is finished. Do you realize it's almost noontime? Come along—we can't spend all day in this grocery store. The door's over here beside this basket of winter pears. Don't tell me these are the sugar pears, the ones that ripen up sweet as honey? That's exactly what they are. Have you ever tried them baked, stuck with cloves and basted with brown sugar? But we must not linger over these pears. Let's step out onto the sidewalk and breathe in the sharp autumn air. Nothing like oxygen to stimulate the brain.... Say, I smell spices. Aunt Phoebe must be making pickles. That's her mustard pickle. She does it with cauliflower and green peppers. She always donates several jars to the church supper. That reminds me, they're holding a supper in the basement hall this evening. Let's stroll past the church and see if there is any sign of....Why yes, the ladies are arriving already, carrying in baskets, napkin-covered baskets, filled with Parkerhouse rolls and brown crocks of beans still hot from the oven. I think we had better cross over onto the other sidewalk, away from all those temptations, otherwise I won't get by the church without going in. Then I would never get this talk done. Let's hurry on down to the waterfront.

It is too bad we haven't a fishing rod or we might join the others who are fishing for smelts. That is what we all do at this time of year, and I don't mean just the youngsters.... If you've once eaten smelts, rolled in corn meal and fried in bacon fat....Oh, but here we are at the government wharf. The tide is in. The wharf is lined with fishermen today, young and old, perched on the very edge, leaning against the posts, dangling a line into the swirling current. See that kid over there by the lighthouse? He just had a bite. It was no smelt either. It almost jigged the line out of his hand. I believe he's caught a codfish, not a tommy-cod, a real cod! That boy's mother will have fresh cod for supper tonight. It will be cooked until it falls to pieces in snow-white flakes. While the cod is cooking she'll be frying up some pork scraps, sizzling them to a nice crisp brown. Then she'll add the cod and some diced up turnips and an onion.

Say, it's not a codfish he caught; he's hauling in an eel! Is he going to throw it back in? That lovely big eel....No, of course not. His mother will be serving eel stew for supper. Did you ever eat eel stew? No, but perhaps you had eel pie? No, well you haven't started to live, have you....

I wonder if he would sell us that eel, so we could have an eel pie? Oh, but then I am not eating anything until this blessed talk is finished.

Look, I'll just have to get out of town, away from all these distractions. I can't keep my mind on my work. Let's make for the railway station; the evening train is due in about now. It's my last chance. We are not stopping by the cider mill. I don't care if they have been grinding out apples all afternoon....What kind of apples did you say? Russet? Northern Spy? No, no, you'll not entice me inside that cider mill. One glass of sweet cider would be fatal. We're catching the first train out of town. Now, keep walking.

Here we are at the station. There is still time to buy a ticket. Uh, one moment please ... while I step over here to the freight shed to take a look at these twelve-gallon barrels. Hm, just as I thought. One is addressed to me! What's in it? Why, oysters—oysters from Malapeque Bay in Prince Edward Island. A friend of mine sends them to me every fall. When I open one of them I can almost see the white boats of Malapeque Bay cutting across her choppy waters to the oyster beds under a blue October sky....For this is the season of the oyster harvest.

You like oysters, of course. Well then, grab hold of the other end of this barrel, and we'll lug it between us....Talk? What talk? Oh, that. I can't think of anything to say. Come on let's have some oysters—on the half shell.

"Let's make for the railway station..."

The Secret Prosperity of the Annapolis Valley

In the summer of 1964 the *Toronto Globe and Mail* carried a story about the Annapolis Valley. The heading read: "Nova Scotia's Valley is Canadian Showcase" and told of driving along the main highway, *mile after mile, through towns and villages strung like pearls, a glistening length of mansions and cottages, most of them white and seemingly all freshly painted. Climb one of the ridges,* the story went on, *and you look down upon the valley, a countryside dotted with towns, villages, hamlets, and farms in equally perfect condition.*

"...snug farmhouses..."

Now is this true? Is the Annapolis Valley indeed one of the showplaces of Canada? Is it that prosperous?

I've lived in the Valley most of my life. And I must say I agree with this picture of tidy villages and snug farmhouses—it does give an impression of prosperity; prosperity in the old-fashioned sense of a Currier and Ives print, with the big red barn, the lofts bulging with hay, root cellars well stocked with turnips and potatoes, cabbages and apples.

In this sense the Annapolis Valley has always been prosperous. Protected by the wooded slopes of the North Mountain, which

"...a special affection for the growing of apples."

rises steeply like a palisade against the bitter winds off the Bay of Fundy, the rich farmland—some of the best soil in the Maritimes—supports herds of beef cattle and grows what Valley people believe to be the finest apples in the world. Valley people have a special affection for the growing of apples. Every spring they celebrate the coming of the apple blossoms in a valley-wide festival, in which an Apple Blossom Queen is chosen from competing princesses from each Valley town.

On Apple Blossom weekend, the roads are jammed with cars, visitors come from Halifax by the thousands—all of them out to admire the blossoms and catch something of the springtime enchantment of this Land of Evangeline.

Longfellow's famous poem of that name tells the fictitious story of two French-Acadian lovers, torn apart on their wedding day by the cruel circumstances of the expulsion of the Acadians from Nova Scotia. The setting for this poem is the village of Grand Pré, nine miles from my home town of Hantsport. And here at Grand Pré, still only a little village and hardly changed from the days of the expulsion, are held some of the festivities of Apple Blossom Sunday.

The Valley is very much what it always has been: breadbasket to the province...and a good place to live. No one in the Annapolis Valley is starving.

Yet, in spite of all this, many Canadians (and indeed some even here in the Valley) would tell you it was not a prosperous part of the country. Not in the way the Niagara Peninsula is prosperous, or the oil rich farmland of Alberta. Comfortable, yes—but affluent, no.

And so, of course, there are those who are not content with mere comfort. They want more of the good things of life. These can't be had, it seems, without more factories...and bigger payrolls.

There are some quite sizable payrolls [in 1964], notably two military establishments: Cornwallis, a naval training base on the shores of the Annapolis Basin, through whose gates more than 100,000 Canadians have passed; and a permanent air force base in the middle of the Valley, at Greenwood—each employing between three and four hundred of the local people. These bases inject large amounts of federal money into the Valley economy.

Food processing, canning apple juice, beans, and pickles employs upwards of a thousand people; and another couple of thousand find jobs in industries unrelated to the Valley's agriculture, such as the Formex Company near Kentville (now consolidated with Kenwood Mills of Arnprior, Ontario) who manufacture synthetic fabrics; an elastic factory a few miles outside Bridgetown; and within the town, a distillery. In Hantsport, the Jodrey Companies have a pulp mill supplying the raw material for the Keyes Fibre Company that manufactures paper plates and egg trays.

Among the Valley's 65,000 people there are those who enjoy working in a factory, and would like to see more and bigger factories. The Valley's Associated Boards of Trade are always on the lookout for potential industries and seek a closer trading relationship between the Atlantic Provinces and New England.

There are, however, those who don't enjoy working in a factory, who are constitutionally allergic to punching a time clock. If they had the chance to stay on the farm and make a fair living, this would be their choice—rather than the prospect of being on shift work around the clock, even with a special bonus for overtime. Though the sidehill farm may have provided little enough in the way of luxuries...it has always provided security. During the depression years, when there were soup kitchens in Toronto and Montreal and Winnipeg, we had no soup kitchens in the Annapolis Valley. I think that is something we should not forget.

The Valley people do not have to turn to factories. They have another string to their bow. The Valley farmers have lived on the home farm, where they and their ancestors for six and seven generations have lived, albeit simply, at times sparely, and even meanly—but lived. Independently.

[There have been significant demographic changes in the Annapolis Valley since this piece was aired. The Cornwallis Naval Training Base has been closed and there have been cutbacks and downsizing in the air force and other military establishments. On the other hand, many new industries have been established in the area.

The Valley towns continue to attract returning Maritimers, retired people, and those hoping for a quieter way of life.]

"The setting for this poem is the Village of Grand Pré..."
Memorial Church and Evangeline monument, Grand Pré.

Some Maritime Mysteries in Stone

The first crossword ever published was in the *New York World* of Dec. 21, 1931. Some thought the crossword would be just a passing fad...but it really caught on. The daily crossword, or acrostic, satisfies our nagging determination to find the answer to a mystery.

Now, I would like to mention some Maritime mysteries that have come down to us, carved in stone. Some have still to be solved, but others are now mysteries only to those who do not know the answer.

In the latter category are the two heads carved in bas-relief which you will find just inside the front door, when you step into the Royal Bank in Windsor, Nova Scotia. Even some of their customers are not quite sure why those sculptured portraits are there, set in the wall. So, here's the story: Windsor used to have a bank of its own, called the Commercial Bank of Windsor. On each side of the door were the carved heads of two of the bank's officials—A.P. Shand, its president, and John Keith, its vice-president. Later on, this bank was taken over by the Royal Bank. A few years ago, when the Royal decided it needed new premises, they saved these effigies from the entrance to the old building and had them placed in the new building. It is surely the only bank in Canada...where the president and vice-president are there to greet you at the door as you come in to cash your cheque.

In our next case, the carved stone was also included in a wall—much to our regret today. At Granville Ferry, on the shores of Annapolis Basin, a certain Dr. Jackson, a geologist, had come from Boston in the year 1827. While making an examination of the area, he came on a very perplexing stone. It was a stone that bore the symbol of the Freemasons—the square and compass—along with the date, 1609. Dr. Jackson was about to take the stone back to the States to present it to the Pilgrim Society of Plymouth—and it's a pity he didn't, because then we'd have it today. But Judge Haliburton, the author of *The Clockmaker*, heard about it (he was living in Annapolis at that time) and prevailed upon Dr. Jackson to let the stone remain in Canada.

Haliburton gave this stone to Sir Sanford Fleming who took it to Toronto...and left it in the care of the Canadian Institute. Through the carelessness of someone at the Institute it was used by some Masons—perhaps because it bore those Masonic emblems—while an addition was being built to the Institute. So this fascinating stone is now quite lost to us. And we can only speculate on how it came to be found in Granville Ferry.

You may recall a television special called "Chariot of the Gods," from a book of the same name written by the Swiss author Erich von Daniken. He claimed that the ancient gods of long-dead civilizations were, in fact, visitors from another planet.

In British Columbia, they have recently uncovered evidence to support this theory—some early pictographs (or rock paintings). One especially looks very much like a being from outer space, with a one-piece tunic, radio antennae, and a spherical helmet fitted with a visor.

I mention these B.C. paintings because we have some pictographs at Kejimkujik Lake on the border of Queens and Annapolis counties, in Nova Scotia. Here the Mi'kmaq, centuries ago, produced a very extensive display of art that goes on and on for several miles. The pictures are drawn, or carved, on ledges of rock in the lake, which are only slightly above water level. Most of the time, this art work is underwater but if the summer happens to be exceptionally dry, the water lowers like a curtain, revealing decorative carvings of ships and birds, animals and people.

The late Dr. Arthur Kelsall of Annapolis Royal, an expert on aboriginal pictographs, felt that some of these drawings represented the Vikings who, as we now know, had settlements in North America as far back as the year 1,000 AD. But, in the light of von Daniken's theory about space visitors, it might be worth re-examining these rock carvings to see if perhaps the figures are fitted with radio antennae, spherical helmets, or other garments useful in space travel. Who knows, the Chariot of the Gods may have visited Kejimkujik...and certainly they couldn't have chosen a more beautiful spot to land.

Wells

The long dry spell of this past summer [1965] reached even into the Maritimes, which ordinarily receives an abundance of moisture. It brought into sharp focus the need to conserve our resources. Water shortages and pollution are problems that are unfamiliar to most Maritimers. We enjoy one of the continent's finest water supplies largely because we are for the most part a country-dwelling people, a relatively unindustrialized people. Our little towns are surrounded by forests and a wilderness of lakes and streams, bogs and swales where the ducks gather—miles and miles of bushland with not a house to be seen. This is the reason our lakes and rivers are uncontaminated.

Every summer, thousands of ex-Maritimers visit their hometown, or the folks back on the farm. Among those who return to my home town, Hantsport, many feel that their vacation is not complete until they have made a trip out to Gullen's Brook to have a drink of its clear spring waters, bubbling up out of a bed of gravel. Or perhaps they make a pilgrimage to Eldridge Settlement, which is now a run-out field of yellowing brown-top, a few dying apple trees, hummocks where the houses used to be...and some old wells. Around the foun-

Old well and willows, Grand Pré, NS. (circa 1913)

"...trout in the well..."

dations grow sweet may and farewell summer, a lilac bush, some waxberries, and tansy—tansy that grandmother used for poultices and for tansy tea.

The wells are filled with sticks and poles where boys have been prodding to see if they can reach bottom. They've loosened a few of the old mossy stones, and plunged them into those dim mysterious depths. Great-grandfather rocked that well up himself. The curbing is gone now. There was once a tidy well-house with a hatch cover and the well pole, with its forked end. All this has gone but there's still water there. How many buckets of it have been carried by members of the family who came here morning and night, as to a little shrine to draw sustenance from the earth? It is all so simple, so uncomplicated, so direct a relation between man and his earth.

Now, a child brought up in the city knows nothing about wells. He turns on a tap. Out comes the water. The source of it is unknown to him. Even grown men in cities look upon the water system, when they see the street being dug up, as a thing of great complexity, with its labyrinthine network of pipelines, the rattle of air hammers, and vast water mains laid bare.

What they are assured of is that the water they drink is clean and safe. It has been filtered, decontaminated, treated in every conceivable manner to render it fit for their consumption. When they come out to the country and find people drinking from a well, they shudder. I have seen city folk refuse to drink well water because they say, "Oh, it's probably contaminated." Everyone today has grown so very sensitive to these things.

The discoveries of Pasteur and Lister, who showed that cleanliness could prevent the spread of infection and that contaminated water was a carrier of disease, made the public very germ-conscious. We are still mortally afraid of microbes, but the fact is that most micro-organisms are quite harmless. If this weren't so, country residents throughout the Maritimes who obtain their drinking water from wells would be dying off like flies because there is no well that is not to some extent contaminated.

Take the matter of cooling the milk down the well, which used to be a popular method of refrigeration on farms that could not afford an ice house. There was always the chance that some milk would escape into the well, and make the water unfit to drink. Farmers were aware of this danger. On some farms, they maintained a special well just for cooling the milk. Others dealt with the contamination problem by installing a trout in the well which became so completely tame that he basked on the surface, opening and closing his finny mouth, and occasionally snapping at a dragonfly.

The quality of the water was determined before the well was even dug—sometimes by that very remarkable man, the dowser, who walked about holding onto a forked alder stick until some electric force drew the end of it down toward the earth. Then he knew that here was a never-failing spring of pure water.

Now the novice would search for water in a low-lying piece of ground, in swampy land, but this is a poor place for a well. Among farmers there's a saying: "The higher the land, the greener the grass, and the better the water." A well on top of a mountain supplies cleaner and better water than at the foot where it gets the wash and the runoff, where the land is muddy and stagnant.

Substantiation for this can be seen at the northern side of the Annapolis Valley. The farms here at the foot of North Mountain, all the way from Blomidon to Granville Ferry, obtain their water from wells up on the side of North Mountain. This water is piped into the houses and barns by gravity, and is delivered with about as much force as most water systems in town. It runs indefinitely and with no water meter and no tax.

Here is borne out another old farmer's saying: "A good water supply is worth half the price of the farm." These wells may be contaminated, but as far as I can see the people in the Annapolis Valley are living into as hearty an old age as any of us.

What some of them are complaining about, or were, during the long drought of this past summer, was that the wells were running dry and that they had to haul water from a nearby lake or river.

This may not mean any significant lowering of the water table. Rather, it may

"The farms... obtain their water from wells up on the side of North Mountain."

" ...underwear ...rinsed once, and then hung out on the line ..."

reflect a change in our way of living. Years ago, when that well was dug and stoned up, perhaps by your great-grandfather, life was much simpler. When he undertook to mop down the top buggy and get the worst of the mud off the dashboard, he may have used two buckets of water. How much do we use washing the car?

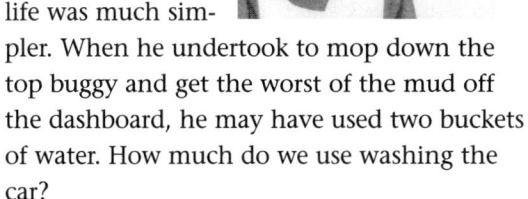

In those days, people had a bath on Saturday night. They didn't luxuriate in the tub every night of the week, and there was no such thing as a shower which can easily do away with a great deal of water.

People did not think of watering the lawn. A lawn took its chances. The idea of watering the grass, of putting out sprinklers on the lawn, was a novelty that would have puzzled or amused our great-grandparents. We have become great users of water, extravagant users of water, and so, of course, we suffer at the very time when our water resources are shrinking.

Today, because clean sheets and towels, white and sparkling, have been held up as a status thing, housewives think nothing of rinsing the clothes out three and four times...and this soon lowers the well.

In great-grandmother's time there was no such thing as a washing machine—unless it was one of those hand-operated washing-machines that must have given her such a thrill. But it did not give her such a thrill that she wanted to haul in three or four changes of wash water. She was satisfied to get the clothes washed in a decent, respectable way. She didn't aspire to make them the fleeciest, the whitest wash of anybody in the neighbourhood.

People wore those clothes, and were perfectly happy, and went to church in the simple pride of one whose underwear has been rinsed once, and then hung out on the line to dry.

Swimming in Minas Basin

You'd like to go for a swim. Well, you could not have come to a better place. Here, in Nova Scotia, we have over five thousand miles of coastline. The distance you would have to hike, if you undertook to explore all of Nova Scotia's bays and headlands, is about the same as the distance from St John's, Newfoundland, to Victoria, British Columbia.

Do we have swimming? Well, just about everywhere you look. So, tuck your bathing suit under your arm and follow me. We're off to the beach.

Here we are at the village of Grand Pré, on the shores of Minas Basin. At least it used to be on the shores of Minas Basin, until three hundred years ago when the shoreline suddenly moved and left Grand Pré several miles inland.

How did this happen? You see, the French Acadians, who first settled this area, were great hands at building dykes. They pushed out dykes against the inrushing tides and dyked off miles and miles of this rich alluvial marshland. So, I'm afraid we have another three or four miles to go. If we walk out, it will give me time to explain a little what these dykelands are. This immense field we're crossing, this great flat stretch of grassland, is the same as you will find in dozens of places about the inner reaches of the Bay of Fundy—all of them monuments to the prodigious industry of the French pioneers. These seacoast prairies have been built up from sediment brought in by tides sweeping up from the Gulf of Maine. As cropland it cannot be beaten, especially for hay. Smell that clover and timothy we're passing through.

You suffer from hay fever? Let's hurry on then; the beach cannot be far away. I believe we are approaching the outer dyke. Yes, see that big grassy mound, standing like a rampart against Fundy's tumbling seas?

"The tide is out..."

That's the dyke. It didn't take us so long did it? Now we scramble up over the dyke and jump down on the other side...and here we are on the beach of Minas Basin. Just look at that expanse of water...er...mud. Oh dear, I was afraid this would happen....The tide is out.

Where has all the water gone? Out there beyond the mud flats. Here, take the binoculars. You may be able to see it, if you adjust the glasses for long-range vision. No, that's not sunlight shining on the water; it's sunlight shining on wet mud flats.

You'd *still* like to go for a swim? It's a long walk out over those mud flats—about another three miles. If we got out there and the tide started to turn....It rises fifty feet you know and comes in pretty fast....Suppose we just stay here on the shore and look for precious stones? You never saw such a shore for precious stones as Minas Basin. Why, we have agate and amethyst, jasper, cat's eye, opal, not to mention obsidian, chalcedony, and quartz crystals in every shade of green and blue.

You are not interested in geology? You would rather go swimming? Well, I'm afraid we are just going to have to wait till the tide is in a little closer to shore. In the meantime, I know what we can do. I'll take you for a walk along the beach and show you one of the few submerged forests in Canada. I can show you the stumps of trees, which grew in the later part of post-glacial times. They are really great monarchs of this "forest primeval." Some of the stumps have as many as two hundred growth rings....

You don't want to see our submerged forest? You just want to go swimming. Oh well, let's just sit down on this old log and I'll recite Longfellow's "Evangeline." The tide should be high enough for us to go swimming by the time I reach the last canto.

"You would rather go swimming?"

Flood Tide

Across a swirl of covered beach
Pale dories creep from mist.
The wavelets drip like far-off speech;
The winging seagulls twist.
My dog sits like a silken mound
And gently rubs my knee,
Lifts ears at all the width of sound
And sniffs the coming sea.

Alan Creighton

Wolfville's International Festival

Russia's world-renowned Bolshoi Ballet is scheduled to tour Canada this coming June [1972]. They will play to glittering audiences in five major cities—in Vancouver, Toronto, Quebec, Ottawa, and Montreal, where they will play at the luxurious Place des Arts.

They will also be performing in Canada's Atlantic seaboard province of Nova Scotia, in a little town called Wolfville. It's a college town, seat of Acadia University, which is the town's main industry.

Acadia is only a small college, with about 2,500 students. About the same number of people live in the town itself, many retired. That is Wolfville, deep in the heart of scenic and uncluttered Annapolis Valley. So why does the Bolshoi Ballet include this little country town in its Canadian tour?

Perhaps for a change of pace. In Montreal, the dancers will be put up at luxury hotels, they'll be taxied back and forth between hotel and theatre, but in Wolfville they'll live in one of the college residences. They will perform, for three evenings, in the college gymnasium.

The ballerinas will eat at the campus cafeteria. Out on the rolling lawns, under towering elms, they'll have a chance to unwind, to look about them and admire the green-tufted pasturelands stretching away to the Bay of Fundy. There are white-faced cattle grazing in the fields, and miles and miles of apple orchards lie just beyond the town limits. This is orchard country.

It is a quiet place, Wolfville, a place most Canadians haven't even heard of. From now on, chances are they'll be hearing more about Wolfville and the festival which, this summer, will headline Russia's Bolshoi Ballet and Lillian Gish, star of the silent movies.

It is not easy for a little country town to attract stars of that stature, but it can be done. It can be done if you're truly stage-struck, and have the gift of communicating your excitement to others.

Jack Sheriff, a professor of English at Acadia, gathered a group of the townspeople around him two years ago, and told them of his dream to

"...a place most Canadians haven't even heard of."

"...he began negotiations for... the Red Army Chorus."

make Wolfville a festival town that would bring star performers from all over the world in one glorious week of theatre.

This is what he told them: "I've been in love with the theatre ever since I can remember," he said. "I can't think of anything more exciting. It brings people together. It's the warmth, the meeting of friends, the live contact, so different from the shadow-world of TV. And then—what a setting for it!"

The idea caught fire. An organization was set up and incorporated—Theatre Arts Festival International—which they shortened, by using the initials, to the catchy name of TAFI. Sheriff decided that if they were going to make it they'd have to start off with a bang in the first season, so he began negotiations for the two hundred voices of the Red Army Chorus.

The price was over $30,000. Who was going to put up that kind of money? The bank would not lend it to them without collateral. One of the TAFI supporters signed a note for $1,000 and then went out and canvassed his friends throughout the Annapolis Valley until he had found thirty others willing to sign notes totalling $20,000.

Meanwhile, Jack Sheriff was on the phone calling Boston, to see if they couldn't get pop singer Joan Baez. When she heard the Red Army Chorus had been signed up, she agreed to come for a fee that was ridiculously low, scarcely more than expenses—provided she and her mother were given front row seats to the Red Army performance.

That is how the Wolfville festival got off the ground: the Red Army Chorus, a bit of help from Joan Baez, along with a great deal of local involvement. People donated their time, their gas. They addressed envelopes, made posters, helped with the advance sale of tickets, opened their homes to entertain the visiting artists, and drove them to and from the airport. The merchants along Main Street and the farmers out in the Valley donated dozens of eggs, chickens, turkeys, bottled pickles, apple cider, and heads of lettuce to help the Social Committee stage after-the-show receptions. The mayor of the town, Mayor Murdock MacLeod, pitched in and helped man the box office.

And it has been a success. During festival week between twenty and twenty-five thousand people will crowd into this little town. They will come from all over Atlantic Canada, from the New England States, from New York, from parts of Canada further inland. They will come here to participate in a cultural *smorgasbord* that provides something for every member of the family—Judy Collins for the blue jeans set, that was last year [1971], or Czechoslovakia's Black Box Theatre for both children and grownups, or the Royal Winnipeg Ballet, or Juki Arkin the Israeli mime, or the Jamaican Folk Singers. It's all part of TAFI, the Theatre Arts Festival International that turns this little town of Wolfville, Nova Scotia, for one thrilling week, into a great celebration of the magic of theatre.

"...front row seats to the Red Army performance."

[TAFI ran in Wolfville from 1970 till 1982. Jack Sheriff, remembering those heady days, adds that one of Joan Baez's conditions was that her performance be an open-air concert. When people suggested it might rain, the reply was "It never rains on Joan Baez." Such proved to be the case. After three days of rain, as Joan arrived by fire-truck on the crowded hillside above the Gaspereau Valley, the sun came out.

The Bolshoi Ballet returned to Wolfville in 1974, the year of Barishnikov's defection to the West.]

Wilmot Spa Springs

If you go into the woods at twilight, when all is quiet, and stand near a running brook, you will hear words coming from the water. It sounds as if someone is laughing, then speaking. Sometimes the voice seems so close you can almost distinguish what it is saying. Thus it was that the old-time Mi'kmaq obtained a great deal of information. It was these voices that told them to go to a certain spring near the little village of Wilmot, in the Annapolis Valley.

Long before the white man set foot on this continent, the Mi'kmaq had paid a yearly pilgrimage to the springs at Wilmot and witnessed the miracle of men cured and made whole again simply by drinking the waters, or bathing in this mineral spring. It is a spring that is so deep it is said to be bottomless. No one has ever had a line long enough to feel the attached weight touch the bottom.

Of course there is nothing new about the healing and tonic powers of bathing. To this very day, in the city of Bath, in England, you can see the astonishing and ornate baths left by the Romans and walk the streets of a city whose follies and gaiety made a glittering chapter in the age of Henry Fielding, creator of *Tom Jones*. Later, Jane Austen's characters could often be found "taking the waters."

It was in 1817 that a gentleman who had visited Bath travelled through the Annapolis Valley. He was told about the springs at Wilmot and went to see them. He tried the waters, and was convinced that they contained this magic substance that, back in Europe, drew thousands every year to visit the spas. The owner of the land, Farefield Woodbury, began to look upon the springs with a new interest. Perhaps the Mi'kmaq were right. Were the tales of miraculous cures imaginary or, perhaps, real?

Already the springs enjoyed a certain fame throughout the district. There were those willing to swear that their ailments had been cured by a visit to Wilmot Springs. All that was needed was some better accommodation which Mr. Woodbury undertook to provide, piping water into buildings where one could take either hot or cold baths.

From that time until the close of the nineteenth century, Wilmot Springs ranked as one of the most fashionable and popular spas on the continent. People came from the New England States, from Niagara, in what was then Upper Canada, from Los Angeles, New York, Philadelphia, and Chicago...and they enjoyed themselves. As one group from Boston wrote in the visitors' book, "All were delighted with the beauty of the scenery, and benefited from the healing properties of the waters."

In August of 1831, a vessel from Eastport brought passengers from various parts of Maine to drink the waters and wander through the five-acre grove of virgin pine laced with paths that led to rustic seats. Here the ladies reclined and flirted a fan as they observed some of the other guests who strolled through this sylvan retreat. Here came the great libertarian, Joseph Howe, and his political rival, the Honourable J.W. Johnson. Over there was the Honourable Samuel Cunard, dreaming of a steamship that would link England and America. Here came Stephen Wiggins and his daughter, from Saint John, chatting with Nova Scotia's Lieutenant Governor and his lady, the Earl and Countess of Mulgrave. There was Judge Haliburton, musing about the creation of a new adventure for Sam Slick, in *The Clockmaker*.

Some of the stories of the cures which were said to have occurred are rather hard to believe. For instance, it was said that an older soldier with a peg leg made of cork once bathed there and the flesh grew upon the cork leg until no one could tell which leg was made of cork and which was real.

Sam Slick was openly sceptical. The Yankee clock pedlar tells of a man in his seventies, so full of rheumatism he could hardly move between his chair and his bed. He made his son take him to Wilmot Springs, travelling in a gig between two mattresses. He was so hopeful that he would be made young again that he planned on getting married when he returned home.

There were tales of people cured of the King's Evil (scrofula). Another story was of a man on his way to Halifax to have a cancerous ulcer on his breast removed who was advised to stop at the springs. He applied lint soaked in spring water to the sore and was cured. A young man in the militia who had a badly infected wrist was sent home to Middleton to die. The local doctor told him to "take this old tin over to the springs. Fill it up with spa mud and get your ma to put mud poultices on that arm. That'll fix it." The young fellow followed the instructions and recovered.

How much of this was fact and how much was fabrication, it is impossible to say. We do know that the public flocked to Spa Springs for the best part of half a century and supported a rambling three-storey hotel with cupolas and upper and lower verandahs. Between 15 and 20 servants were employed there.

The social elite of the day came to Wilmot in the summers, to Spa Springs. They would have taken occasional trips over to the Bay of Fundy in carriages hired from a livery stable, trotting up over the mountain to Margaretsville, Port George, and Port Lorne.

Life at Spa Springs passed peacefully from one sunny day to another. There were fresh buttermilk, fresh eggs, new peas, and salmon from the Bay Shore. Is it any wonder that spirits and appetites revived?

Then, suddenly, it all came to an end. In 1889, the Spa Springs Hotel was destroyed by fire. Although later efforts were made to

"Here the ladies reclined and… observed some of the other guests…"

exploit the springs, none of them succeeded. By 1900, the idea of a spa in the Annapolis Valley was just a memory.

The spa everywhere in America had had its day; it was not something that just happened here in the Maritimes. Spa therapy was an idea transplanted from Europe, but it had never really taken root—even though for a time it had become something of a fad. For a while, except for Saratoga in New York, and the polio treatment centre at Warm Springs in Georgia, nothing was left of what was once almost a way of life.

This seems very odd, in a way, because we are such a fun-loving people. For people so dedicated to youth and amusement, it is strange how grimly we cling to our hospital cards, our Canada Health cards....Our wan little faces seem forever pressed against the window of a hospital begging to be let in. Illness is too serious a business to be cared for in these gay and carefree resorts where the patients loll in the sun, take baths—and expect to get well.

Whether those people I told you about actually did get better, whether cork legs were thrown away as real legs recovered, does not really matter. What matters is that this way of life, among the grove of towering pines, with picnic carriages bucketing off to Margaretsville on the Bay Shore, with Joe Howe chatting amiably with the leader of the opposition, could never have happened in a hospital...but only in a spa. It was Wilmot Spa Springs with its deep bubbling waters which once brought such gaiety, such effervescence, and such therapeutic good cheer to the Annapolis Valley.

Bridgetown

If you haven't yet decided where you're going for your vacation, I have a little plan that might appeal to you. I suggest you forget about jetting over to Europe, or cruising down to Barbados and, instead, spend your vacation in Bridgetown.

Now the reason I suggest Bridgetown is that I've just been reading a fascinating book all about Bridgetown, written by Elizabeth Ruggles Coward.

There is only one thing wrong about Mrs. Coward's book. It gives the history of the town up to the year 1900—and then it stops. There is nothing after 1900. That limits my knowledge of the town to Victorian times. So...if you don't mind packing your portmanteau and boarding an exciting train called *The Flying Bluenose*, we'll journey down the Annapolis Valley to the Bridgetown of 1895.

Now, as you step off the train, you'll notice how Bridgetown has providentially been located on one side of the Annapolis River with the railroad on the other, so that the town is not dissected by a string of squealing freight cars, as in so many towns.

The cabby loads your portmanteau and straw trunk into the front seat of the barouche. Away you go at a brisk trot, but not for long. In a moment you'll be crossing the bridge after which this town is named. As you approach the bridge, you see a three-masted schooner tied up at the wharf and realize that Bridgetown is a port with access to the Annapolis Basin and the Bay of Fundy. Packets run a regular summer schedule up to Boston and over to Saint John. This vessel loading lumber is the *Nancy Anna*, with her captain, John Longmire.

Now you have almost reached the bridge—known as the Old Red Bridge. Over the top, in large letters, is a sign bearing these instructions: "Keep to the left...and walk your horses, or you will be fined."

"...spend your vacation in Bridgetown."

Well, you finally get safely across the bridge and you're on your way to The Grand Central Hotel at the head of Queen Street. It is a first-class hotel with three stories, a cupola, balconies, and an appreciative audience waiting on the front verandah. Mrs. Coward describes that front verandah in these words:

The chairs were invariably occupied by men who seemed to have nothing to do. With hats on their heads, chairs tilted back and feet on the front railing, they surveyed the hapless females who passed by. Tongues wagged faster there than in the Ladies Sewing Circle. Old timers in the town have an ineradicable memory of that well-filled lower verandah of the Grand Central Hotel.

The things they saw from that verandah! Back in 1881, they saw a bicycle driven down Queen Street, one of those old velocipedes with the high front wheel, called a penny-farthing. Then, the *Bridgetown Monitor* says that, *quite a sensation was caused in our streets the other day by the advent of one of these iron horses brought here from Boston by Mr. Melbourne Hardwick, a stepson of D. Nicholls of Clarence. The small boys followed the machine in droves as long as they could keep up with it.*

Granville Street, Bridgetown, NS circa 1890.

Not until 1897 would the first motor bicycle make its appearance on the streets of Bridgetown—a machine of English manufacture, driven by Kenneth Skinner and capable of going 25 miles an hour!

But this is only 1895. Before we get swept away in the madcap age of the motor bicycle, let's linger awhile among the buckboards and buggies and pretty cut-unders. Bridgetown was famous for its carriage factories. There were five of them. A particularly smart dreamboat was generally given a write-up in the *Monitor*, something like this: *A handsome and stylish side bar three-quarter buggy was made for the Rev. H. D. DeBlois by Arthur Palfrey*. It is possible that you may be able to get a picture of that buggy—that is, if you brought your box camera along with you. I hope you did. You will want to take some pictures out at the Trotting Park. Tomorrow night there will be a game between the Bridgetown Cricket Club and the Wanderers Cricket Club from Halifax. You'll want some pictures of that!

Don't forget that on Saturday evening, at Victoria Hall, you'll be able to take in a Quadrille Assembly put on by the True Blue Baseball Club. A Quadrille Assembly, in case you didn't happen to know, is a dance.

Of course you could not get to know all the people of Bridgetown in these few short weeks of your vacation. But you will meet some of them and find them very interesting people, in many ways quite unusual. They are descendants of New England Planter stock and United Empire Loyalists. Among them are several families who belong to the Society of Friends, in their broad-brimmed hats and wide Quaker bonnets, the people of friendly persuasion. Ever since the town received its name in 1824, it has shown an abiding concern for education and the things of the mind. In 1826, they established their own library, the Bridgetown Reading Society. They have had a public school since 1824 and, thirty years later, we find several private schools, including a Select Academy for Young Ladies and the Clarence Seminary for Young Ladies. Here the young women are instructed in drawing, music, arithmetic, geography, and astronomy.

In the school registers are the names of these old Bridgetown families: Hicks, FitzRandolph, Vidito, Troop, Fitch, Ruggles, Chesley, Piper, Chute, Foster, Morse, Fowler.

You'll get to know them, if you come back again for your vacation next summer—in 1896.

A Visit to Annapolis Royal

Many years ago, before there were bridges over most of the rivers, a great business was done in ferrying people across from one side to the other. At the mouth of the Annapolis River, a rowboat plied back and forth between Granville Ferry and Annapolis Royal, directly across the water. The man who ran this ferryboat employed one of his servants to do the actual work of ferrying passengers across. One day, a gentleman appeared on the Granville side wanting to cross over to Annapolis. However, he said that unfortunately he had no money with him.

The ferryman said, "Well, but all it costs is sixpence."

"I know," said the man..."but I don't have sixpence."

The ferryman was now in a ticklish situation. He did not want to refuse a well-dressed gentleman like this, but, on the other hand, he had orders to always obtain his fare before allowing passengers aboard. Finally he said, "I tell you what, boss, a man that ain't got sixpence is just as well off on this side of the river as he is over in Annapolis Royal."

That may well have been the case back in the 1700s...but not so today. There are good reasons for wanting to cross over from Granville Ferry to Annapolis Royal. This is especially true at the time of Annapolis Royal Natal Day festivities. These days of celebration are to remind us that this little town, nestling securely behind the grassy ramparts of Canada's most historic fort, Fort Anne, was once the capital of Nova Scotia, which then included New Brunswick as well.

It is no longer necessary, of course, to use a ferryboat to cross from Granville Ferry to Annapolis Royal. You can drive, or cycle, from one side to the other across the causeway. Right here, before you even enter Annapolis Royal, is a good reason for coming. If you happen to like bass fishing, you could not find a

"...to cross over from Granville Ferry to Annapolis Royal."

"...spring water from a pipe at the side of the road."

more convenient spot for casting your line than off the causeway at Annapolis Royal. They have taken bass here weighing as much as thirty pounds.

I will admit there is one good reason for remaining on the Granville Ferry side of the river. That reason is the never-failing spring on the road to nearby Parkers Cove. A few years ago, I rode over to Parkers Cove by bicycle...or rather, I trudged up over the North Mountain, pushing my bicycle most of the way. When I was halfway up the mountain, I was able to quench my thirst with sparkling, unchlorinated spring water from a pipe at the side of the road. They tell me it runs continuously, summer and winter. People drive up here from the Valley, to the road over to Parkers Cove, to fill up jugs and even barrels with the clear, cool water that comes gurgling out day and night. It forms a little brook that goes tumbling down the mountainside.

But now, let's hurry back to Annapolis Royal....As you come in off the causeway, turn to your right. This will bring you to the lower part of St. George Street. Here, you will find a most unusual monument to private enterprise—to the enterprise of a group of citizens who undertook on their own initiative, with limited funds, and doing much of the actual work themselves, to save and restore several historic buildings from possible demolition...and they were successful!

Operating on a restricted budget from donations and from money-raising activities such as rummage sales and the sale of second-hand books, this group, who called themselves

"...acquired and restored...the O'Dell Inn and tavern."

"St. George's oldest house…the Banks House…"

Historic Restoration Enterprises, first acquired and restored an old inn—the O'Dell Inn and Tavern. It is now open to the public as a museum.

Then there is the McNamara House next door, said to have housed the first school in English Canada. Built in 1780, it has been completely restored, including the old classroom where you can examine a fine collection of early schoolbooks. Another building, the Pickles and Mills Store, contains a craft shop and exhibition of costumes and various utensils of the period. All of this was accomplished by a group of private citizens, working on their own.

Where else would you find a street like St. George Street? Dreaming under wine-glass elms, its old houses help to recall an age of crinolines and red coats, the warmth of great chimney corners, spacious dining rooms and gracious living.

On St. George Street, a house is not considered grown up until it is at least a hundred and fifty years old. It comes into the full bloom of its charms after passing the two-hundred-year mark.

St. George Street's oldest house is the Banks House, which is further distinguished by having a ghost. There, a strange woman haunts one of the bedrooms, wearing a checkered shawl and restlessly rocking herself in a rocking chair. When word of this first got abroad, the old folk around town recognized the description and shook their heads! It was Mrs. Barclay who had once lived here and, according to local rumour, had been cruel to her slaves. One horrifying story has it that a slave was murdered and sealed up in a fireplace, with Mrs. Barclay's ghost returning to rock uneasily at the memory of the crime. If this is true, there must be some other ghosts moving about in dormered bedrooms along St. George Street, for this is not the only story of the mistreatment of slaves.

One of the town's historians, Charlotte Perkins, tells of slaves tied up by their thumbs in the attic, and of a slave girl who had stolen a pie being made to crawl into the hog-pen to retrieve and eat the crust she had thrown there. These, one would think, deserve some fairly restless ghosts.

If you want to savour something of this erstwhile capital of Nova Scotia that has been quietly holding the fort and defending a heritage that goes back over three hundred years, plan to take in the Natal Day festivities.

[This piece was broadcast in 1977. The O'Dell Inn and Tavern remains as described but the McNamara House (renamed for historical accuracy, the Robertson House) is now a private residence. The Pickles and Mills Store has been sold and is being made into suites.

The present owners of the Banks House, situated near the Historic Gardens, assure us that the ghost has been laid to rest; nobody has used that bedroom rocking chair for years. Annapolis Royal still celebrates its Natal Day on the first Monday of August, and each fall, an Arts Festival is held, sponsored by the Annapolis Regional Community Arts Council.]

Sandy Cove

Last summer, a friend from New York spent her vacation here with us in Nova Scotia. While in the province, she took in all the usual tourist spots—the fort at Annapolis Royal, the Habitation, Blomidon and Scots Bay, the Lookoff, Peggys Cove. These were days of strenuous sight-seeing, but these were not the days she remembered.

In a letter we received recently, she talks not about the Habitation or the picturesque fishing villages, but about a certain afternoon we spent with some neighbours, sitting out on the riverbank, just doing nothing.

She says, *I still remember so vividly the afternoon with your neighbours out on the riverbank, watching the tide coming and going, the seagulls, the boy flying his red kite, the peaceful quietness. It was nice but so short. Whenever the noise and the confusion of the people around me are too much to take I always think of Nova Scotia, your street, the few people around. What luxury!*

Now this is nothing new. For over a hundred years Americans have been coming to the Maritimes as an escape from the rigours of metropolitan living. The thing they are looking for, that special quality, is summed up in one word—quietness.

It was the same back in 1923 when a book was published, called *Ambling Through Acadia*. It is something of a collector's item today. The

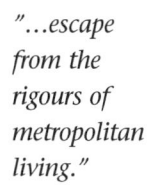

"...escape from the rigours of metropolitan living."

author was Charles Hanson Towne, another New Yorker—by profession a naturalist, by inclination a poet.

In this book, as in so many others written by Americans about the Maritimes, one theme keeps recurring, like a strand in a woven tapestry: their fascination with the serenity of our way of life, and the contentment which they seem to find here. This is how Charles Hanson Towne describes some Nova Scotia fishermen:

Some of the old fishermen along the shore are as handsome as cardinals, and quite as dignified; and all have the eyes of dreamers—that indescribable peace on their countenances, which you do not see in city-bred folk.

Notice the quality that wins his admiration. It is not the perky energy of the go-getter, the driving clamour of industry. What he is looking for is the tranquillizing calm of an afternoon on the riverbank, or at a place like Sandy Cove.

Let's follow Charles Hanson Towne as he ambles along through the province. Having arrived in Yarmouth on the Boston boat, he travels up the French Shore by train, stopping off here and there to rent a bicycle and explore the countryside. He learns of Sandy Cove on the other side of Saint Marys Bay. As he cycles through Weymouth, he stops at the bridge to talk with one of the inhabitants and to inquire about the best way of getting to Sandy Cove. The man on the bridge smiles tolerantly and wants to know why anyone would be anxious to see a place like Sandy Cove. *"A dull little place," was the way he put it. Nothin' doin' at all.* Charles Hanson Towne adds: *It would have been folly to explain that was the very reason I wanted to get there.*

Now Sandy Cove is not like other coves. This gem of a village has been sought out by artists and writers and discerning tourists. For generations they have been raving about it, but quietly, for fear of bringing on a stampede of idle sightseers. So far it has not been overrun because of its location. It is off the beaten track, halfway down Digby Neck. A trip to Sandy Cove means returning some twenty miles on the same road in order to get back onto the main highway. Most tourists do not bother to pay it a visit, which is just as well, because the charm of Sandy Cove lies in a certain seclusion and an air of long, unhurried summer afternoons.

Charles Hanson Towne charters a motorboat and chugs across the Bay. He says he will never forget his first sight of the village...*snug and quiet, as if it had purposely folded itself away in those hills, aloof from the clamour of the world. It was too wonderful to be true, finding this white, clean, sleeping little town on a day so golden and calm.*

As he strolled through the village, he noticed something about the people who lived there. *Each one that I met seemed happier than any one I had seen in a long time. I remember a youngish man who was painting the fence around the cemetery of the Church of England who, jubilant at our enthusiasm for his native place, said to* us, "You're right, I guess. You won't find a prettier spot in the whole world than right here." He said it simply, not vaingloriously. I knew he loved every inch of that brown road that was the main street of Sandy Cove—loved it with all his heart; and I liked him for feeling that way. It wasn't a case of every goose being a swan to him; it was the normal pleasant pride of one who knew that fortune favoured him by setting him down in this green-white village to spend his days; and he went on brightening that picket-fence which held in a close brotherhood the silent dead who had once been as happy as he in Sandy Cove.

Notice how this author conveys the sense of quietness so welcome to city folk even back in those days. This is in 1923. They minded the noise in New York even then. What a joy it must have been to discover that there was such a place as Sandy Cove.

"This gem of a village..."

He continues, *No harsh noises for dear little Sandy Cove! It is still with a beautiful stillness; and the only excitement of the day seems to be the arrival and departure of a motor-bus that travels over the hills to Digby, twenty miles away. A jitney they will stand for, but no railroad, no movies, lurid and false.* Then he adds these few verses to complete his picture:

The little town of Sandy Cove tucks itself away
Between the warm Canadian hills, beyond Saint Marys Bay;
And there it dreams through lazy hours the whole long summer day.

The little town of Sandy Cove is beautiful and white.
No railroad thunders at its heart; no windows flame too bright;
No movies flash their garish signs, "A Thrilling Show—tonight!"

But quietly the little town sleeps and nods and smiles.
It lets the noisy world go by with all its ways and wiles,
Content to watch from its high hills the distant Happy Isles.

Would I might dwell in Sandy Cove in peace and calm, and say,
"Good-by, fond, foolish, clamouring town! Good-by for many a day!"
And nestle in those sheltering arms beside Saint Marys Bay.

[Charles Hanson Towne continues on his journey. He is following the spring north to the white apple orchards, which await him in the heart of the Annapolis Valley around Wolfville and Grand Pré. His book *Ambling through Acadia*, with its elegant illustrations by W. Emerton Heitland, is long out of print but worth searching for in antiquarian bookstores.]

"...the silent dead...in Sandy Cove."

PEOPLE

People

The first peoples must have rejoiced in the bounty of land and sea which they found in the sheltered Annapolis Valley and it is no wonder that the Mi'kmaq god, Glooscap, is said to have established his home on nearby Blomidon (named Cape Blow Me Down by early explorers).

Successive waves of peoples, Acadians, Planters and Pioneers, Loyalists, and remittance men, came to make their living in this fertile place. They were followed by more modern immigrants—people from Europe after the two world wars looking for cheap land for farming; army, navy, air force personnel, and war brides. Representatives from all these groups are to be found in Norm's radio essays. He was curious about what brought people to the area and how they made a living.

Norm was interested in genealogy and, time and again, we find he returns to the theme of inheritance. He feels that a sturdy pioneer background gives rise to a people who are independent thinkers and who are resourceful and inventive, such as Alfred Fuller of Fuller Brush fame, and inventors, Charles Burgess, Abraham Gesner, and Errol Shand.

As a writer, Norm was fascinated by other writers and by what inspired them. He himself made few attempts at fiction, though it seems he would have liked to have been able to write a novel. So we can appreciate how he enjoyed the opportunity to meet or correspond with Ernest Buckler, Lynn Cook, and Joyce Leslie.

An amazing parade of diverse personalities marches through Norm's essays, from William Hall, the hero, to Bucknam Pasha, the would-be hero. They may have all—or nothing—in common. We should just enjoy them as they are presented, appreciating that Norm never passed judgement on any one.

Then and Now

Many of the people who settled in the Annapolis Valley are Connecticut Yankees, who came up from New England two hundred years ago, drawn by the inducement of cleared land that could be had for a shilling for fifty acres.

For five years after the expulsion of the Acadians in 1755, the farmlands had remained vacant and silent, the hay uncut, the apples frozen on the branches, until the coming of these New England "Planters" as they were called. They were of Puritan stock, some of them descendants of the Pilgrim Fathers—Jonathan Graves, Elnathan Palmeter, Prudence Chipman, Deacon Iliakin Tupper, Abigail Rand, Seth Burgess. From Nantucket and Lebanon and Martha's Vineyard, New London and Plymouth, they began trickling into the empty townships with spinning wheels and looms, and canopy bedsteads, and with a stern devotion to righteousness.

Listen to one of their preachers, Pastor Henry Alline, as he addressed the New Light Congregationalist Church at Cornwallis in 1781: *Brethren, this week gone...I went from Cornwallis to Horton...and oh how was I grieved to see a vast crowd of people at horse racing! Oh, if they knew the worth of those precious hours they are wasting, they would not risk their souls on such a pinnacle of danger!*

Along with their grandfather's clocks and warming pans, these New England Planters brought with them much of the Puritan austerity. Even today, in the vicinity of Berwick, there are those who think twice before reaching for a pack of cards.

Memorial outside the United Baptist Church, Falmouth, NS

They took their religion very seriously. I was shown a house in Bridgetown that is known locally as the Faith House. It came to be so named because of a cripple who once lived in Bridgetown, a little girl of 16, confined to a wheelchair and with no chance of making a living, but with an abiding faith that some day she would own a home of her own. She prayed that this might come to pass, and the innocence of her faith was so compelling that the congregation banded together and built her a house. It became known as the Faith House, and over the front door she had printed "In God We Trust."

They brought something else with them, these New England Planters: a sturdy independence of mind—because independence was the very bedrock of Puritan belief or Congregationalism. It was their belief that each congregation is locally governed and only answerable to itself. You'll find today this same crotchety air of independence among Valley people.

They've produced some quite independent thinkers. Abraham Gesner, inventor of the oil lamp and the process used to manufacture kerosene oil, was born at Cornwallis. Alfred Fuller, of Fuller Brush fame, came from a village near Centreville.

"But what of the coming generation?"

The Valley won an approving chapter in Rachel Carson's controversial book, *Silent Spring*. Valley apple growers had chosen to challenge the need for complete reliance on pesticides. The man who led them in this greater emphasis on biological control was Dr. A. D. Pickett. Though a New Brunswicker, he had found in the Annapolis Valley the climate and opportunity for a new look at insecticides.

It's a place that encourages a new way of looking at things. Novelist Ernest Buckler, in his novel *The Mountain and the Valley*, has given us his own, unique picture of the country and its people. Buckler lived alone on his 140-acre farm, which overlooked the Annapolis River, a few miles outside Bridgetown. He was independent enough to do his own cooking—and had (as I discovered), an artist's touch in creating an omelette.

We've been talking about those who have achieved things. But what of the coming generation? What are the teenagers like here?

To find out I had a phone conversation with Robin Steeves who teaches at the

Bridgetown Regional High School. He tells me the youngsters there are exceptional in their stability. "I have never," he said, "seen a school with so few disciplinary problems as in Bridgetown."

It was the same story further down the Valley, at Annapolis Royal, where I spoke with one of the high school teachers, Mr. Clark, who comes from Jamaica and so is able to appraise the children from the vantage point of a non-Canadian. They strike him as reserved, well mannered, but behind all this good behaviour some are ready to confess that they are bored to death with life in Annapolis Royal.

Indeed, I can't help sympathizing with them, for there is absolutely nothing to do in Annapolis Royal. There is no bowling alley, no poolroom, and no coffeehouses. There is only the Friday night dance at the Community Centre and the galling realization that it was here, in Annapolis Royal, that all the action got started back in 1605, because this was the birthplace of what later was to become Canada. There is hardly anything you can mention they didn't do first in Annapolis Royal: the first water-powered grist mill, the first Roman Catholic Church, the first social club, the first theatrical presentation. Today [1968], all they have is a second-run movie on the weekends.

Why, the centennial train didn't bother to stop at Annapolis Royal. I spoke to a woman who saw it go through at quarter to seven one morning. She was one of the few people in Annapolis Royal who caught a glimpse of the centennial train as it whizzed by on its way up the Valley to Kentville. It didn't even slow down.

Things like this make the kids in Annapolis Royal feel they've been left out of it—that there's no chance for them here. They feel they have to get away, go to Ontario, or down to the States.

But if they do leave, they'll be leaving a house that has been in the family for generations, that hasn't had a mortgage on it since great-grandfather's time, where their parents and the rest of the family live rent-free, paying country taxes, where they are able to reduce their grocery bill with a kitchen garden and some fruit trees, a few hens and a cow. Here a family on a low income is still able to live decently...comfortably...even graciously.

"What are the teenagers like here?"

SIDEHILL FARMERS

There used to be a lot of folks living back on the mountain on scrabbly little hillside farms, with one or two raw-boned cows and a pig or two. They lived in weather-beaten shanties with roofs of tarpaper; the wind blew in under the eaves and hens ventured in over the threshold, pecked about on the kitchen floor right up to the stove where Granny sat mumbling on a clay pipe.

We all smiled and said, "Well, those are mountain people. That's how they live."

Well, Granny's gone now. The little shanties are all painted white. They've shooed the hens out the back door where they can now roost on a two-tone convertible that's parked out in the yard. It is a real classy job, missing a hubcap and some grillwork, but watch her climb those hills. That's mountain folk, 1968-style.

But the funny thing is that all of a sudden everyone's starting to talk about these people, and not saying very nice things either! After the poor souls have gone to work and

"...it has cost someone...a lifetime of work..."

improved themselves, brushed themselves off and bought a washing machine, the same as everyone else, you'd think we'd congratulate them, give them a medal or something. But no, that is not the way we do things. Our standards are pitched pretty high these days. The sight of some unregenerate farm wife still drawing water from a well sends Ottawa into a flurry of statistics; we are asked to give a moment of quiet thought for the Guernsey cow that must sleep in an unpainted barn.

You've heard the talk; you've read it in the newspapers. Rural slums, they call them—pockets of poverty. Apparently we here in Nova Scotia are among the worst offenders of all. Isn't it terrible?

What are the authorities going to do about it? Well, they talk about moving these people to other places, giving them jobs in a factory, educating them.

Maybe the people don't want a job in a factory. Maybe that kind of education doesn't appeal to them. Maybe they'd like to stay on that little farm, where they were born and raised, and know every stick and stone within shooting distance, and perhaps have kinfolk on those other farms just over the hill. Maybe they're a lot happier than you think they are.

Let's be honest. We don't care two pins if they're happy or not. It's us we're concerned about, not them. We're worried because these little shanty people haven't any money. They don't buy things. Why, they can't even get in debt to a loan company! You can't have that kind of thing going on.

What I find disturbing about it all is the casual way we talk about moving these people off their farms, as if they were digits in a ledger to be lifted from one page to another, to show a profit for the rest of us.

There's a saying here in Nova Scotia: "Talk's cheap, but it takes money to buy a farm." No matter how small the farm may be, it has cost someone years, perhaps a lifetime, of work, and thought, and patience, and love—love of every stone-infested field and hollow, the chattering brook, the grassy swale, of every undrained swamp.

These people have paid for their farms. And who can say for sure what it all means to them? They may derive from their way of living a sense of freedom which we may never know. They may even enjoy a more downright self-respect than those hundred-dollar a week men in the factory, so dear to the heart of every economist.

LANDSCAPE

Below high domes of mellow cloud
Some shadowed trees are nodding;
A ploughman swings along, dark-bowed,
With heads of horses plodding.
Far off, the blue horizon weaves,
A glint of ocean showing,
While nearby are the curl of leaves
And homestead roses blowing.

Alan Creighton

Grand Pré Revisited

They were cousins from New Brunswick, both poets: Bliss Carmen and Charles G. D. Roberts. Both loved the tidal country of the Bay of Fundy and its swirling, muddy waters, and some of their finest inspiration was drawn from the marshlands.

During the 1890s, either one of them might have been seen wandering across the dykeland at Grand Pré, notebook in hand. Their haunting portraits of the countryside were written by men who had time to dream, to indulge in the luxury of contemplation, unencumbered by television, or radio, or the sweet inducements of the motor car. Afar off would sound the faint tinkle of ox-bells or the distant whistle of a train pulling into Wolfville station—that represented the headlong pace of progress.

We looked on life and nature
With eager eyes of youth,
And all we asked or cared for
Was beauty, joy, and truth.[1]

How quiet it all seems...how leisurely. Yet behind those distant ox-bells was being carried on a way of life that had very little time for poetry. What were the people of Grand Pré thinking?

There was, for example, Nathanial Faulkner, who owned a farm in North Grand Pré on what is known as Long Island, and maintained a herd of 64 head of cattle. He and his wife were an aging couple, creeping up into their 80s, and they had one hired man, a young lad not out of his teens.

"...in North Grand Pré..."

The day began at four o'clock in the morning, or sometimes three-thirty if there was marsh grass to be mowed, because you had to mow the marsh grass while the dew was still on it. Once the dew dried off, your scythe would become dull after one or two strokes.

But this is just an ordinary day. Four o'clock…and the faint flickering glow of candles can be seen in the upstairs rooms of all the farmhouses in North Grand Pré. Mrs. Faulkner made her own candles out of tallow which she rendered from beef suet. The hired man was given special consideration. He had an oil lamp in his bedroom.

I heard the spring light whisper
Above the dancing stream,
"The world is made forever
In likeness of a dream."[2]

A lantern's yellow circle of light sways across the barnyard and disappears into one of the buildings. The chores have begun. They are milking the twelve milk cows, then forking hay into the mangers, feeding the animals in the fat cattle stable, who require turnips from the turnip pulper, cracked grain, and some cornmeal.

Then the cattle are driven out of the buildings and down to the watering-trough where they are watered, all 64 of them, the water being pumped into the trough by hand.

Breakfast is at 6:30, followed by more chores with a short break for dinner. Then, for variety, there may be a spell with the bucksaw until about half past three, when it is time to begin the evening milking, feeding, and watering.

At evening, where the cattle come to drink,
Cool are the long marsh-grasses, dewy cool
The alder thickets, and the shallow pool,
And the brown clay about the trodden brink.[3]

By 8 p.m., the chores may be finished. The woodbox has been filled with stove wood, kindlings cut for the morning, water drawn from the well and carried into the kitchen. Now it is time for the hired man to pick up his beautiful oil lamp, the one with the pink roses on it, and go to bed…unless he feels like playing a game of dominoes—but that would generally be just on a Saturday night.

Let me taste the old immortal
Indolence of life once more;
Not recalling nor foreseeing,
Let the great slow joys of being

Well my heart through as of yore!
Let me taste the old immortal
Indolence of life once more! ₄

Now, Mr. and Mrs. Faulkner were a kindly old couple; they were not slave drivers, but there was no time for indolence in their way of life. In those days at the beginning of the twentieth century, in order to exist, in order to make a farm pay, it was necessary to work 15 hours a day. You did not sit around after a meal and relax. You picked up your cap and went outside and started working again, greasing the wagon wheels, mending the harness. You might have the job of threshing the grain on the barn floor with a flail. Then the grain was carted over to Hunter's grist mill in Gaspereau, and ground into flour for another year's supply of bread and buckwheat pancakes.

Black on the ridge, against that lonely flush,
A cart, and stoop-necked oxen; ranged beside
Some barrels; and the day-worn harvest-folk,
Here emptying their baskets, jar the hush
With hollow thunders. Down the dusk hillside
Lumbers the wain; and day fades out like smoke. ₅

One season chased after another. Summer was in some ways the easiest time, when the cattle were out on range on the dykes. It left the farmer free to sow twenty acres of oats, put in a kitchen garden, spread manure from the 64 head of cattle, and get the barn linters filled up with fresh hay of his own cutting.

Tons upon tons the brown-green fragrant hay
O'erbrims the mows beyond the time-warped eves,
Up to the rafters where the spider weaves,
Though few flies wander his secluded way. ₆

Eight hundred barrels of apples had to be picked every fall, and hauled off to the fruit warehouse in Grand Pré. After that came the fall ploughing. Soon the cattle were brought in off the dykes, and once more there were the chores to be done.

When the ruts in the cart-road ring like steel
And the birds to the kitchen door come for their meal,
And the snow at the gate is lightly drifted
And over the wood-pile thinly sifted,
Oh, merrily shines the morning sun
In the barn-yard's southerly corner. ₇

Snow is gusting over the shaggy backs of the oxen. They sway forward in the starlit dimness of early morning, their heads yoked tightly together. The hired man is on his way to the woodlot. The bobsleds move slowly across the open dykeland toward the main village of Grand Pré. Then on to the Gaspereau Valley, with Dutch bells tinkling, across Melanson bridge, and up Gaspereau Mountain to the woodlot. It is seven miles...by ox team.

He gives the animals their hay, slackens the yoke straps so they can move their heads, but hardly pauses to light his pipe. A cord of wood must be loaded on, and there is still the long drive back across the dykes. He will be lucky if he gets home by suppertime.

It takes twelve such trips...for twelve cords of wood, and it is a month before all the wood is in the barnyard. Then the bucksaw must be sharpened, the wood sawed and split and packed away in the shed. Then, before the winter is too far gone, they must go down to the dykes to cut ice for the ice house.

When the ice is chopped at the great trough's brink,
(Oh, the frost is white on the latch.)
The cattle come lazily out to drink;
And the fowls come out on the sun-lit straw,—
For the sun's got high, and the south eaves thaw,
(And the frost is gone from the latch.) [8]

So, as spring approaches, another season's work begins, most of it done by this one hired man. What does he get? Fifteen dollars a month—which was good pay in those days. I believe it was even raised to twenty. Even so, he knows in his heart he will never be able to save up enough to buy a farm of his own. He will always remain a hired man, following someone else's plough. At times he too must have his dream of what he might have been.

Make me over, mother April,
When the sap begins to stir!
When thy flowery hand delivers
All the mountain-prisoned rivers,
And thy great heart beats and quivers
To revive the days that were,
Make me over, mother April,
When the sap begins to stir! [9]

[The quotations are from: [1] Bliss Carmen, "The Enchanted Traveller;" [2] Bliss Carmen, "Earth Voices;" [3] C.G.D. Roberts, "Where the Cattle Come to Drink;" [4] Bliss Carmen, "Spring Song;" [5] C.G.D. Roberts, "The Potato Harvest;" [6] C.G.D. Roberts, "In an Old Barn;" [7] C.G.D. Roberts, "In the Barn-Yard's Southerly Corner;" [8] C.G.D. Roberts, "The Farmer's Winter Morning;" [9] Bliss Carmen, "Spring Song."]

WILLIAM HALL—V.C.

The Victoria Cross is named after Queen Victoria and was instituted by her at the end of the Crimean War, in 1856. It is a simple bronze cross, bearing the royal crest and words "For Valour"...I believe the citation reads for "conspicuous bravery in the presence of the enemy." No other medal is so universally honoured. It is a fact that [in 1980] Canada's highest proportion of V.C.'s had been awarded to Maritimers —four in Nova Scotia, three in New Brunswick and one in Prince Edward Island.

One of these men was born only a mile or so from Hantsport at Horton Bluff. Yet, his name—William Hall—you will not find in any list of Canadian Victoria Cross holders. The reason is simple—when William Hall was growing up, going to sea as a boy, and later joining the British Navy, there was no such country as Canada. William Hall was proud to call himself a Nova Scotian, for it was in Nova Scotia that his parents found freedom.

They were black and lived at a time when slave ships still plied their grisly trade between Africa and America. William Hall's father was aboard one of these slave ships when she was captured by the British Navy, towed into Halifax, and her human cargo released.

His mother also escaped from slavery because of the British Navy. During the War of 1812, the city of Washington was under attack by British forces. British ships had sailed up the Potomac River almost to the capital itself. William Hall's mother managed to smuggle herself aboard one of these ships. By the time she was discovered, they were at sea, bound for Halifax...and freedom.

From childhood on, William Hall was taught by his parents to revere the British Navy and the White Ensign as the symbol of freedom. All during his boyhood he dreamed that some day he would serve in that British Navy and perhaps help someone else escape to freedom. He was to meet just such an opportunity during the Relief of Lucknow.

How did it happen that William Hall, serving in the British Navy, would find himself in 1857 at the Relief of Lucknow—a city in the middle of India? The Indian Mutiny had aroused the British public to the point where no one could talk of anything else but the gar-

"...For Valour..."

rison at Lucknow. It had been under siege for more than four months; its 1,700 inhabitants, including women and children, were facing the same fate that had already overtaken the fallen garrison at Cawnpore...massacre.

Troop reinforcements hastened from Hong Kong. Aboard H.M.S. *Shannon* was Able Seaman William Hall. Arriving at Calcutta, they took to barges, which were towed up the River Ganges to get as close as possible to the interior of the country. Then the soldiers went ashore, with Hall joining this landing party as a volunteer. They fought their way across country to British Headquarters at Cawnpore. From there they were led by Sir Colin Campbell, Commander-in-Chief of British Forces in India, as they pushed forward toward the besieged garrison.

Sir Colin Campbell had at one time served as Governor of Nova Scotia and, by a happy coincidence, the man in charge of the garrison at Lucknow, General Sir John Inglis, was a Nova Scotian. So, it was very much a Nova Scotia day—the day they brought relief to Lucknow.

The garrison at Lucknow was stationed on the top of a hill, surrounded by massive stone walls. There was no way to get through to the defenders unless, somehow, the walls could be breached. It was decided their only chance was to use a 24-pounder siege gun from the *Shannon*—to push this in close enough that its charges could shatter and break through the wall. The gun crew was one man short, and Hall, who was in charge of another gun, volunteered to take the place. "I guess I'll go with you," he said.

"...born...at Horton Bluff."

The gun was rolled into position. Under the concentrated fire of the besiegers, one after another of the gun's crew was shot down until only two men were left alive—Hall and an officer, Lieutenant James Young, who was badly wounded. They kept on, bringing back the gun after each recoil. Hall was now working the gun virtually single-handed. In one supreme surge of determination, he fired the charge that opened the walls at Lucknow and allowed British forces to fight their way to the relief of the garrison.

If you should ever be driving through the town of Hantsport you will see, directly in front of the Hantsport Baptist Church, a monument to this man, erected by the Hants County Branch of the Canadian Legion.

[William Hall is further remembered in the Nova Scotia Museum and at the Black Cultural Centre for Nova Scotia in Westphal, where exhibits commemorating his life and achievements can be seen.]

"...in front of the Hantsport Baptist Church, a monument..."

The Truth About Men of Iron, Ships of Wood

We view it all through a veil of romance. The ships were beautiful; the voyages, sagas of courage and endurance, of roistering sailors, and sea shanties. The reality, which was very different, lingers dimly in the memories of a few old salts who can still remember what it was like to go aloft and furl the sails in a gale of wind.

I've talked with these men. Some of them were friends of mine. When I was a youngster, the little Nova Scotia port where I live, Hantsport, was filled with retired sea captains. There were also men who had spent a lifetime in the fo'c'sle and retired simply as able seamen—but able now only to wander down to the wharf and lean up against a snubbing post, sunning themselves and remembering.

These men carried for us children a peddler's pack of wonders. They told of the China Sea and of wintry crossings on a sleet-driven Atlantic that had left them proud of the part they had played, whether as captains, ship's carpenters, or just plain ordinary sailor men.

They were proud, I think, of the fact that they were tough and could take it. They saw

"...shanghaied from the waterfront doss-houses and grog shops..."

nothing unusual in the pittance they received at the end of their voyage, or in the living conditions aboard ship. What, then, was it really like going to sea on one of those old windjammers?

There were good captains, fair men, according to the standards of the time. But there were others who were not so fair; these are the ones we don't talk about when we recall the stories of the wind ships.

There were, indeed, some captains who rather enjoyed making the lot of the men as miserable as possible. They operated on the principle that if things were tough enough, the food scrimpy and monotonous, the men would jump ship at the first opportunity, thus relinquishing their wages which the captain put in his own pocket.

Sailors had a name for it. They called it "running men off the ship." No seaman would wittingly sign on with such a ship, so what these captains did was this. They sailed down to Boston or New York with a skeleton crew from the homeport who were paid off, except for the officers, and given a ticket back home to Nova Scotia. Then a fresh crew was shanghaied from the waterfront doss-houses and grog-shops, and by the time they reached Pensacola, Florida or Cardiff, Wales, they were ready enough to run away from the ship and forget about their wages. Another crew was rounded up, some of them so drunk they were hauled aboard with a heaving line, and it began all over again.

These were the ships where the hard-driving bucko mates ladled out plenty of "handspike hash" and "belaying-pin soup" for shirkers or mutineers. These were captains who won such titles as Black Taylor, Devil Summers, and Hell-fire Slocum.

The notorious Captain Larsen of Jack London's novel, *The Sea Wolf*, was in real life a man from Cape Breton, Nova Scotia. He never forgave London for having written those things about him. But his principal objection was not that he had been depicted as brutal but that he had been killed off in the final chapters, after a sound licking.

As one old sailor man said to me the other day, as he reminisced about those great days of the wind ships: "It's a lost art. And a good thing it has been lost."

"...those great days of the wind ships..."

Sea Morning

Below the heavy grind of clashing street
The weathered dreamers come. A schooner lies
Where May is nodding, promiseful and sweet.
They watch with light of hungry-happy eyes
A curve of solid deck that freely lifts
A rhythm of masts against a sky of blue.
Along with lulling swell is mingled drifts
Of murmurous harbour-talk: "She's overdue…"
"Bill tells me that the *Minnie A*. got off…"
And wistfully they glimpse an easy flow
Of leisured foam across the open trough
Within the dock. The idle warmth of sun,
The slender cry of gulls, the briny air
Is full of roving-urge, of hawser-strain,
While, lolling aft, a boy with golden hair
Is humming low a chanty's deep refrain.

* * *

The tide and morning wait! We can depart!
The weight of city years is swept away
And strength has come to every sailor heart
With longing stirred beside a sea of May!

Alan Creighton

The Man From Noggin Corner

You know what it is like to look forward to hearing from someone at Christmas, someone very special. The card doesn't come...and you begin to wonder....Is it something you said?...Have they changed their feelings about you?...Why isn't there something in the mail?...Perhaps it is just the Christmas rush....You wait...and then New Year comes. Still no card, no letter. You can almost feel the indifference....

Well, there was a young man whose feelings I could be describing, who lived in a little community close to Wolfville. Today it is called Greenwich, but back when this story takes place, in 1809, it was called Noggin Corner because at that time there was a small factory there that manufactured quarter pint wooden mugs, or noggins—the kind you drank your West India rum out of.

This young man, Ebenezer Bishop, wasn't thinking about any noggins of rum. At 25, he was a very sober young man, and the situation he found himself in did not lend itself to celebration.

During the previous summer he had taken passage on a schooner and sailed across Minas Basin to the other shore. There, at a little place called Halfway River, which today is Parrsboro, he became acquainted with a family by the name of Lewis, and had fallen hopelessly in love with their eldest daughter, Anna, a girl of 18.

In the evening, the family would gather about the great fireplace and Ebenezer was made to feel as welcome as one of their own children. The boys lay near the fire roasting apples and cracking beechnuts. Mr. Lewis sat in the huge master's chair, puffing on his long churchwarden pipe, while Anna bent over the little wheel spinning flax, and glancing every so often at the young man from across the water.

Ebenezer chided himself. Why had he not spoken up then and asked her to be his bride? But he hadn't. Perhaps it would have been too much to expect her to come so far across the Minas Basin to live on his Annapolis Valley homestead with his mother and father, when she was clearly so fond of her own family. Once across the water she would see very little of them. Yet he knew that other men in his position would have asked her. Now...perhaps it was too late. There would certainly be other suitors from along the Parrsboro shore. One might have to travel far to find such a girl as Anna Lewis. In those pioneering days a man could not face the toil of clearing the land for a farm all alone. He must have a wife. Perhaps,

"...a Christmas message from Anna Lewis..."

by now Ebenezer had lost his chance.

Then something wonderful happened! On the Monday of the first week in January, in this year of 1809, a belated Christmas message arrived at Noggin Corner, from across the bay. It had gone overland, 57 miles on horseback from Parrsboro to Truro, 65 miles by coach to Halifax, 45 miles by coach to Windsor, 15 miles on horseback to Lower Horton, over bad roads covered in deep snow and finally arrived at its destination. It was what Ebenezer had been waiting for—a Christmas message from Anna Lewis, folded and sealed with a great round red wafer.

As Ebenezer Bishop broke open the seal, his heart was filled with a wild rapture. She had not forgotten him. Her name was still Anna Lewis. There was still time to present himself and plead his case. But how much time? Would she still be unengaged by next spring when the Minas Basin would once more be open to sailing ships?

It was then that the young man hit upon a bold plan. Word had reached Noggin Corner that the ice packs were now jammed in the Minas Channel between Cape Blomidon and Parrsboro. The three miles of water were now a wilderness of ice cakes, rough, hummocky and continually shifting with the swiftly running Fundy tide. No one had ever attempted to cross on this ice before. No one even knew if it was possible...Ebenezer Bishop decided to find out.

Two days after receiving Anna's letter, Ebenezer drove out to Blomidon to see the ice for himself. He took one man into his confidence, Nathaniel Loomer of Scots Bay, who tried to discourage him from this foolhardy plan, but Ebenezer was determined. Across the ice to Cape Sharp was three and a half miles. He stepped out onto the ice and began walking.

With nothing but a board to help him, he attacked this desolation of pack ice—a clutter of ice cakes with here and there patches of open water. Under his feet, he could feel the force of the tide pushing and shoving at the ice, loosening the ice cakes and rolling them over so the mud-stained underside was upright. You could hear the ice growling. Sometimes he was driven a quarter mile off course to escape open water.

The night before, a light snow had fallen and this had hidden some of the joints between the ice pans. At one point he stepped onto what appeared to be solid ice and felt it beginning to sink under him. He threw himself flat on his face, caught the notched board over a hump of ice and began to claw his way upward onto a firmer ice floe, slopping freezing water all over its slippery surface....

Several hours later, Ebenezer Bishop stepped ashore near Cape Sharp, climbed the cliff and started on the twelve mile tramp to Parrsboro. Within a few hours he had proposed to Anna Lewis and been accepted.

Three days later, he started on the return journey to the Annapolis Valley—this time on horseback, for his bride-to-be would not hear of his risking his life again on a second crossing of the ice.

They were married the next fall, in October. She wore a dress of red taffeta. The material had been brought from Halifax the year before.

As far as is known, this is the only time anybody has ever crossed over from Cape Blomidon to the Parrsboro shore on the ice. The honour goes to that earnest young suitor from Noggin Corner, Ebenezer Bishop.

"...drove out to Blomidon to see the ice..."

The Man With a Curse on His Field

I'm not going to mention his name because he was not a very nice person and, since some of his descendants may still be around, why mention it? It is strange how we keep quiet about these things, how reluctant we are to say anything unpleasant about our neighbours and friends. (We can say nasty things about politicians but not anyone else.)

This provides the evil man with a convenient screen, behind which he can hide his shifty and acquisitive operations. Nobody says anything. We're all so well mannered, following the advice: If you can't say anything good about someone...don't say anything at all.

Evil men, down through the ages, must have chuckled over that one as they plunged ahead from trickery to double-dealing, knowing that, unless they ran afoul of the law, their bad deeds would seldom be brought to public attention.

"...Planters...took up land near Port Williams."
Jenny Sheito, oil copy of an unsigned painting.

But in the case I am talking about, the man badly miscalculated public opinion, which has remembered him for some six or seven generations...as the man with a curse on his field. He was a farmer, who lived in the Annapolis Valley, near Port Williams. At that time it was not Port Williams but was known as Terry's Creek, a little settlement alongside the Cornwallis River.

Let's call him Ichabod, a good old Puritan name, for his folks had come from New England. They were Planters—as were most of the original settlers who took up land near Port Williams. They were an industrious, God-fearing people, strict in their business dealings, ready to honour a debt to the last penny and just as ready to insist on the last penny that was coming to them. The truth is, there were not too many pennies going around the Valley in those days, very few shillings, and hardly any pounds.

You had to be careful and keep watching out for opportunity. And the most indefatigable watcher of them all...was Ichabod.

Now, it so happened that two British soldiers had deserted from the garrison in Halifax and had been seen travelling in the direction of the Annapolis Valley. Within a week or so, a

"*...the barracks at Town Plot.*"

mounted courier forded the Cornwallis River at low tide, and clattered along the road to the barracks at Town Plot. Within an hour, a notice had been posted, offering a reward for the apprehension of the two deserters—a reward of twenty pounds.

Twenty pounds—for doing nothing more than notifying the authorities. The notice was read, and re-read till every man in the community knew it by heart. All that was asked of them was to inform.

And yet, which man could bring himself to do it? In most of these homes there was little love for the British Army. During the American Revolution there were some, right here in Kings County, in the Valley, who had expressed seditious opinions and even prepared to raise a Liberty Pole. And now, could they, these sons of liberty, terminate the liberty of two wretched deserters from the British Army?

A few days after the posting of the notice, two men appeared out of the woods, dressed in the tattered remnants of what might have been a uniform. They made their way to the nearest farmhouse to ask if they could be spared a bowl of porridge or a slice of bread.

"...he had need of two strong men."

They were not refused. They were fed generously while being asked where they had come from. Their faltered answers proved to the householder that finally he was face to face with the deserters and had the awful responsibility of becoming an informer.

Suddenly, he was overwhelmed with a feeling of revulsion at the thought of the twenty pounds...and the fate that would await these two men. No, no, he had no work for them. They would have to go elsewhere. Try at some other farm.

In the next few days, the identity of these men was soon known to everyone. Along Belcher Street and Church Street, the talk was of nothing else, but not one of the farmers of Port Williams could find it in his heart to turn them in. Yet they hesitated to employ them—to be thought a party to anything illegal or seditious. So the men wandered from farm to farm, begging for food, until they came to the farm of our friend Ichabod.

Ichabod gave them a hearty welcome. Yes, indeed, he had need of two strong men. There was work to be done down on the dykes and if they proved themselves able, at the end of the season he would give each of them a golden guinea.

Ichabod kept his two hired men hard at work all that summer and well into the fall. Then, after the crops were gathered, but before he had paid them the golden guinea, he mounted his horse and started out for Halifax where he notified the authorities that he had the two deserters...and would like his reward.

The two men were brought back to Halifax and hanged at the Willow Tree, near the North Commons. With the twenty pounds, Ichabod purchased a field he had long coveted. The people of Port Williams can still show you that field. According to what they tell me, Ichabod's neighbours were so outraged by what he had done that they put a curse on this field that he had bought with the reward money, so it would never again grow a successful crop.

Bucknam Pasha—A Boy From Halls Harbour

Ambition is found in the most unlikely places. Nobody really knows why some people have it while others don't.

Consider a boy named Ransford Bucknam. He was born in 1865 on Nova Scotia's Fundy Shore, in the little fishing village of Halls Harbour. His people, who were fishermen and shipbuilders, would scarcely have believed that this son of theirs, Ransford Dodsworth Bucknam, to give him his full resounding name, would grow up to become an admiral.

He started out with very little in the way of an education. By the time he was fourteen he had shipped before the mast and from then on the sea was to be his university. Now Ransford Bucknam was only one out of thousands of his contemporaries here in the Maritimes who took up seafaring, and none of them became admirals. Why this boy?

Well, he did not do it quite alone. On his shore leave, in the States, he had met an American girl who completely changed his life. She inspired him to want to get ahead in the world and make a name for himself. The strange thing about ambition is that it sometimes takes a quiet, unassuming woman to provide the ignition that leads on to greatness.

They got married and settled down in the little town of Castine, Maine, on Penobscot Bay. At least this was to be Mrs. Bucknam's home during the many weeks and months that Captain Bucknam was away at sea. By this time, he had his master's papers and each command was more important than the last. Mrs. Bucknam was proud of her husband and how well he was doing. She could not refrain from letting her neighbours know that a big shipyard in Philadelphia had engaged him for a very special assignment; the shipyard had received a contract from the Imperial Turkish Government to build four modern revenue cutters and our hero was to deliver the first one.

The Sultan of Turkey was having trouble with his tax gatherers who

"...the little fishing village of Halls Harbour."

moved slowly about the country on the backs of donkeys, filling their hide bags with tax money which seldom got back to the Sultan. They were often set upon by bandits or, if they managed to gather a really sizable sum, the gatherers themselves would skip across the border and settle down to a life of ease in Rome or Paris. The Sultan decided that something had to be done and figured that the revenue cutters would put an end to all this pilfering.

When Captain Bucknam arrived at the Golden Horn with the first of these revenue cutters, it was something of an occasion. The ship was dressed out with streamers of bunting. Constantinople itself was gay with flags and insignia. The captain soon learned that the Imperial Sultan, Abdul Hamid, with an appropriate entourage, would be arriving at any moment to inspect the ship.

Luckily, the Philadelphia shipyard had provided him with a special uniform, equal to such pomp and circumstance. He rushed back to his cabin and quickly donned the wonderful garment—dress coat with gold eagle buttons and rows of chevrons, white gloves, and a tall hat glittering with gold braid. Thus resplendent, he went out on deck to receive his Imperial Majesty.

With a great blaring of trumpets, the Sultan was escorted up the gangway to meet Captain Bucknam who proudly did the honours, with a proper Imperial salute and a gracious bow. The Sultan inspected the ship and was very favourably impressed—especially by Captain Bucknam's uniform. Before leaving the ship the Sultan proposed that Captain Bucknam should take command of the new revenue service and assume the title of Bucknam, Pasha, Admiral of the Imperial Turkish Navy, with a stipend of $15,000 a year, a magnificent salary in 1902.

Captain Bucknam listened to this offer with a certain air of indifference. He replied that he would consider the matter. The Sultan, fearing he might lose this able and imposing man, hastened to add that the position would command, in addition to the $15,000 a year, a harem of proportions worthy of an Admiral of the Turkish Navy.

Captain Bucknam, by this time, was inwardly so overcome by mirth that he could hardly keep a straight face. He could imagine the folks back in Halls Harbour, when the news arrived that little Ransy Bucknam was now an Admiral with a harem all his own, just like in the Arabian Nights! What he should have been thinking about were the folks back in Castine, Maine, and the girl who had inspired him to make a name for himself.

However, the temptation was just too great. The offer was one which Captain Bucknam found himself unable to resist. In fact he was so excited about it that in a letter to his wife he neglected to mention anything about the harem. He asked her to be sure to address her next letter to Bucknam Pasha, Admiral of the Turkish Navy, Constantinople. It would give

"...he neglected to mention anything about the harem."

them something to talk about in the post office at Castine, Maine.

Mrs. Bucknam was ecstatic. She read his letter at the next meeting of the Ladies' Aid. All the other ladies were made properly jealous and aware of their husbands' deficiencies. She wrote to her husband, suggesting that she should leave immediately for Constantinople to take up her official duties as wife of the Admiral. By return mail she received a hurried answer warning that Constantinople was no place for a pretty young woman like herself. She would have to wear a thick veil and seldom appear out in the streets unless accompanied by her husband. And he was busy, very busy....

Back in her Penobscot Bay home, Mrs. Bucknam fretted. She wrote numerous letters to her husband asking how long this state of affairs was going to continue. Gradually she became aware of a different atmosphere at the Ladies' Aid. It seemed they knew something she didn't and she sensed it was not to her advantage.

Of course it was impossible for Bucknam Pasha to continue this thing indefinitely, keeping his wife in ignorance of the true situation. Constantinople was one of the busy ports of the world and he was too well known in shipping circles. Word of what was going on eventually got back to Castine, Maine.

Now someone among the ladies was so kind-hearted that she just had to tell Mrs. Bucknam all about it, and commiserate with her over her husband's defection. At this point, most women would have given in. They would have sued for divorce, but not Mrs. Bucknam. She was going right over to Turkey to give the Sultan a piece of her mind—him and his harem. Poor Mr. Bucknam must be having a terrible time....Well, she was coming to his rescue just as fast as she could get there.

On the boat, on the way over, Mrs. Bucknam fell into conversation with an employee of the Thomas Cook Tourist Agency, a man named Borillo. He took a sympathetic interest in her story and offered to do what he could, as interpreter, to assist her in reaching her husband.

When they reached Constantinople, Borillo engaged a carriage and he and Mrs. Bucknam drove to the Sultan's palace. Mrs. Bucknam

"...someone among the ladies ...just had to tell Mrs. Bucknam..."

demanded to see the Sultan right away. The palace guards had never experienced anything like this before; they did not know what to make of it. She was refused admittance but was given directions to the naval headquarters. Here they encountered more guards. Mrs. Bucknam's shrill voice now angrily called for her husband but the guards explained he was not there. Where was he then? Probably at his harem. Further directions were given.

By the time they reached the harem, Mrs. Bucknam was sputtering with frustration and chagrin.

"Listen," she said, "I'm the American wife of the Admiral and I want to see him immediately."

The guard, when this was translated for him, looked puzzled, "American wife; you say? He has one Spanish wife...some French...some Syrian...a few Egyptian...but the Admiral Bucknam Pasha has no American wife. No."

By now she was in a perfect frenzy of rage, and it was only because of the patience and tact of Mr. Borillo that they did gain admittance to an Admiralty waiting room. Here, finally, Bucknam Pasha was to meet his wife.

What she told him during their private interview, no one ever knew. Whatever it was, Bucknam Pasha was no match for his wife. She left him and sailed on the next boat.

Within a month, he resigned his post as Admiral of the Turkish Navy and returned to their home on Penobscot Bay.

Mrs. Bucknam had firmly established the fact that, in that family, from now on she wore the Admiral's uniform.

The Man Who Put Us on the Map

Will R. Bird's novel *An Earl Must Have a Wife* is a fictionalized account of the life of Colonel Joseph F. W. DesBarres, who was the greatest cartographer of his time. DesBarres never married and never enjoyed the promotion or honours which he certainly merited. He was one of the most unusual men ever to live in the Maritime Provinces; he spent much of his time at his home, Castle Frederick, near Windsor.

DesBarres served with distinction at the first siege of Louisbourg and was with Wolfe at the Plains of Abraham. He served as Governor of Cape Breton (1784 - 1787) and later became Governor of Prince Edward Island (1805 - 1813). He possessed many outstanding talents but it seems that diplomacy was not one of them. He had, as had been said, "a well-deserved reputation for irascibility." This seems strangely out of character, for everything we learn about DesBarres indicates an amiable and rather sensitive disposition. Perhaps because of his Huguenot background, he was sympathetic towards the French. He was ever ready to help an old friend, using his influence to secure a pension for the widow of an old brother officer. His sudden fits of temper hurt no one but himself. Maybe he suffered from gout, that scourge of his time.

Early in his career, for whatever reason, he found his advancement blocked at every turn. At some point, perhaps in one of those London salons where a reputation could be fatally wounded over a glass of sherry, something DesBarres said or did gave offence to a man of influence near the Crown.

It would be 35 years before he was finally raised from the rank of lieutenant to colonel and for a man of DesBarres attainment, this was perpetual frustration. Not until he was 71 did he

"...on his estate in Falmouth, near Windsor..."

"Castle Frederick, of course, is no longer there."

become convinced that the man after whom he had named Cape Breton's most important community, Lord Sydney, was no friend but his personal enemy. Most men would have been destroyed by this faceless opposition, but DesBarres met each new refusal by plunging into work with a fierce and awesome energy, an energy that was to produce the greatest work of map-making in a century of map-making, the 1700s.

At last his talents were recognized by Lord Howe who realized the importance of a survey of the Atlantic coast—much of which was uncharted. This would be important not only to naval vessels but to merchant shipping as well. Under Royal instructions, DesBarres was given the job.

The survey took him ten years. He mapped the coast all the way from the Gulf of St. Lawrence to the Gulf of Mexico. It took him another ten years to compile and edit all this information and see it through the printers. The title he gave this work was *The Atlantic Neptune*. Don W. Thomson, who wrote the official history of surveying and mapping in Canada, calls it *one of the most remarkable products of human ingenuity, determination, and industry to appear during the eighteenth century. The artistic excellence of the sketches is very high and this quality was solely due to DesBarres*. Captain Cook, the famous navigator and explorer, learned his map-making from DesBarres. This was while Captain Cook was stationed at Halifax where DesBarres instructed him in mathematics, astronomy, and surveying. But none of the maps produced by Cook could compare with DesBarres' masterpiece.

The Atlantic Neptune includes sketches of the North Point of Grand Manan Island, of Campobello, Saint John Harbour, and the entire Fundy shore. Volume two shows Nova Scotia's South Shore as well as Halifax Harbour. Volume three charts the harbours of New England. He was the first man to chart the treacherous waters of Cape Sable Island.

The actual drawings were done on his estate in Falmouth, near Windsor, where he had built himself a manor house and named it Castle Frederick. At one time he employed some twenty helpers on this vast map-making enterprise.

Castle Frederick, of course, is no longer there. It disappeared years ago but the property still has links with DesBarres. Descendants of his live on or near the old Castle Frederick estate and two trees remain alive which he had planted— some purple lilacs and an old pear tree. Perhaps it is possible that some papers or maps belonging to DesBarres are to be found in some obscure corner of a Falmouth home.

In addition to his map-making, which must have taken up most of his time, DesBarres managed the affairs of his many farm holdings. It is said that he controlled some two hundred thousand acres in Nova Scotia and New Brunswick. In his farming ventures he proved a good friend to many of the Acadians after the horrors of the Expulsion in 1755, helping a number of them to get re-established. We know from a census, taken in 1770, that Acadians were farming on his land at Falmouth. He helped others get set up around Minudie in Colchester County, NS.

DesBarres was always on the move; in addition to Castle Frederick, he had permanent homes in Cape Breton, in Charlottetown, and Halifax.

Colonel Joseph Frederick Wallet DesBarres died in 1824, at the age of 102, in Halifax. Beamish Murdoch, the Nova Scotia historian, attended his funeral and has left us this account:

I had the honour of attending the funeral of this eminent person on the 31st of October. The funeral procession left his late residence at 3 p.m. His honour Mr. Wallace, the president, most of the members of H.M. council, the gentlemen of the bar, the officers of the army and navy, and many of the inhabitants, attended, by invitation as mourners. This procession was escorted by a detachment of the military, and the rear closed by a number of carriages. On arriving at St. George's Church, in Brunswick Street...the funeral service was read by the Rev. J. T. Twining, and at the conclusion three volleys were fired by the troops.... Rain fell heavily, but the attendance was great, and the interest felt was remarkable....This amiable and valuable warrior was within one month...of 103 years of age when he died.

[While DesBarres never married, he had mistresses on both sides of the Atlantic. One of these, Mary Cameron, and subsequently her daughter, Amelia, managed the Castle Frederick estate in DesBarres absence.]

Charms of Boredom

Did you ever notice that in every community there are always people who spend a great deal of time walking about the streets, but not seeming to get anywhere? They just walk, these people. They keep moving back and forth, around the block, down to the railway station, then into the post office only to reappear shortly on Main Street headed in the direction of the drug store. Having reached the drug store they don't stop, they keep right on going, faster than ever, up past the Community Centre and around the corner by the Baptist church...not going anywhere...just walking.

You don't have to be in town long before you realize that these perpetual walkers suffer from that universal malaise of modern times—boredom. Their lives at home are so excruciatingly empty they can scarcely wait for breakfast to be over before they're out on the streets, walking.

"...a better light to read by..."

Now the rest of us may be just as bored as they are. Come to think of it, a good many of us are, but at least we exercise a certain amount of restraint. We keep our uneventful lives hidden from the full light of day. But these people are quite shameless. They don't sit huddled behind drawn curtains, the way the rest of us do. They make a parade of their boredom. They trail it about town like a child pulling a sled. In the wintertime their bright, glowing cheeks and frosty breath proclaim that boredom agrees with them. They thrive on it! That's what's so infuriating about these people.

The more I think of it, the more I'm forced to acknowledge that boredom may, in fact, be one of the great propulsive forces of civilization.

Consider, for example, a man like Dr. Abraham Gesner, who was born in Cornwallis in the Annapolis Valley in 1797. He was a man of many parts—country doctor, geologist, inventor, the man who founded the New Bruswick Museum in Saint John. In Gesner's day, illumination in the home was by way of tallow candles, or by the use of whale oil and other animal and vegetable oils that had been used for centuries. The lamps were smoky and smelly. Reading by the light of such a lamp was offensive to both eyes and nose, so most householders went to bed at sundown. Gesner, whose lively intelligence made him one of the most remarkable Canadians of all time, found himself faced with an unbearable three hours of overwhelming boredom during those long, smoky, unprofitable winter evenings. So he set to work to give the world a better light to read by, which he did by inventing the kerosene lamp. He moved down to the United States, where his patents were registered, to found the North America Gaslight Company at Hunter's Point, New York. This eventually became part of the Standard Oil Company of New Jersey, owner of Imperial Oil of Canada. In other words, boredom in Gesner's case led him on to an important discovery. It was intellectually profitable.

From boredom has sprung spiritual comfort as well. The Salvation Army came into being because General Booth had discovered that many souls were not being reached by the church. For those faced with real trouble, real heart-searching despair, the regulation church service was too remote, too stereotyped, if it must be said, too boring. These congregational drop-outs just simply didn't go to church. The Christian message passed them by. But, in 1882, the Salvation Army began its ministrations in Canada, in London, Ontario. Five years later, in April of 1887, uniformed men and women, carrying a flag and beating a bass drum, *"entered Bridgetown, NS to set up a Salvation Fort."* The report for that Sunday mentioned it as, *"A blessed day, especially in the evening when three precious people started for the Kingdom, making ten for the week."* The report concludes with this call to commitment: *"Bridgetown for Jesus! shall be our battle cry."*

So, you see, boredom has produced its spiritual, as well as intellectual, fruits.

PASTORAL

The farmhouse skyline, draped with trees,
Is like a summer coast, green-boughed:
The cattle drift on rolling seas
Of luscious field against curled cloud.
They move as lazy ships, wave-borne;
Their bodies glisten sharply red,
With shaggy brow and curving horn,
Large waggling ear, grass-bending head.
With dainty hoof and solemn lurch
They munch along their quiet search.

Alan Creighton

The Burgess Family

A few years ago, if you'd gone to the store to purchase a battery for your flashlight, the chances are you would have bought a Burgess battery. Burgess batteries at one time enjoyed almost a monopoly. Dealers tell me they are not quite so popular as they used to be here in the Maritimes, which is a pity because, in a sense, the story of the Burgess battery began right here in the Annapolis Valley, with a man named Frederick Burgess.

Like many another Maritimers, he felt the urge to migrate to greener pastures. So, he beat his way out to Oshkosh, Wisconsin, where he spent most of his life. He raised a family of three sons who so distinguished themselves in the field of engineering that they were written up in *Who's Who In America*. One of these sons, Charles, had an especially brilliant career as an inventor, along much the same lines as Thomas Edison.

Charles Burgess, or Dr. Charles Burgess as he became later on, set up the Burgess Laboratories, and among the more than four hundred inventions he turned out was the dry cell battery. He established a separate organization, the Burgess Battery Company, a venture which proved highly profitable. He made a fortune and was awarded honours and degrees. Eventually, he became something of a tycoon and spent his last years on an island, on the West Coast of Florida, known as Burgess Isle.

This success is heady stuff. What is the secret of it? Burgess was not the only one from these parts to get ahead in the world, but since Burgess's family background is, in so many ways, similar to that of other Maritimers, let's see if an examination of his origins can provide a clue to his success.

The story begins among the Pilgrim Fathers at Plymouth and Salem, Massachusetts, those dourly righteous men and women who, because of their religious principles, were willing to face the hardships and uncertainties of life in the New World. But determination alone was not enough. In their first winter at Plymouth, half the colony perished from disease, cold, and starvation. Nature ruthlessly applied the pruning hook and left only those strong in both body and faith.

Among those who survived the scarcity of those first winters, was Thomas Burgess who became one of the Pilgrim leaders. He prospered and acquired a section of land in the township of Sandwich, which remained in the family for over two hundred years.

The children and grandchildren of Thomas Burgess gradually spread throughout all of

New England and married into many notable families. Two presidents, General Ulysses Grant and Franklin D. Roosevelt, traced their ancestry back to this man. Sir Charles Tupper was another descendant. We find a Burgess sailing up from Cape Cod and settling on Cape Sable Island. Other members of the family continued on to New Brunswick and took up homesteads along the Bay of Chaleur.

In the Annapolis Valley, two cousins had occupied lands left vacant by the banished Acadians. One of them settled at Newport Landing, on the Avon River, to establish the Hants County branch of the family. At Canning, not far from Kentville, Seth Burgess was granted some six hundred acres and established the Kings County branch of the family, which produced the inventor of our Burgess Battery.

Seth Burgess and his wife, Abigail Howe, brought with them a starchy insistence on religious observance, reflected in the names they gave their daughters: Prudence, Thankful, and Mercy. Although they left the Congregational Church, because of the American Revolution, turning to the Baptist or Presbyterian faiths, they remained as stern and unyielding as ever.

Not long ago, a member of this family recalled what life was like at her grandfather's farm. She says, "Grandfather was very strict. No hot meals were served on Sunday unless grandmother was not well and then she was allowed a cup of hot tea. If the fire went out on Saturday night, it stayed out until Monday. Father said he only remembered it going out twice. It had to be banked very carefully to keep it going."

This was at the home of Stephen Burgess who lived at Lakeville, in the centre of the Annapolis Valley. He was a frugal, hard-working farmer, like most of his neighbours, wringing a meagre subsistence from the land, determined, above all else, that his children should grow up to be good and industrious men and women.

It was his son, Frederick, who took leave of this austere way of life, to seek his fortune in Wisconsin, seeking perhaps not so much his fortune as a bit more fun, gaiety, and romance.

This dream was soon shattered by harsh reality. From a daily diary, which Frederick Burgess kept at this time, we read that he longed "for the

"...one of them settled at Newport Landing on the Avon River..."

home of my birth, the place of all others most dear to my heart." He was homesick and lonely. He worked as a blacksmith's helper, a farm hand, and a labourer in a stone quarry. As he says in his diary, he was "gloomy" when "out of employment, which is the present instance. However, I'll keep up my courage and my eye out."

Always he dreamed of better times coming, when marriage to his Nova Scotia sweetheart, Anna Heckman from Rose Bay, Lunenburg County, would be economically possible.

Eventually, he established himself in the city of Oshkosh, Wisconsin, investing his savings in a grocery store. When word reached him that Anna was visiting her sister at Lynn, Massachusetts, he took the first train back East, and there, at her sister's, they were married. Shortly afterwards, Anna Heckman was on her way out to Wisconsin where she would spend the rest of her life.

"...in the centre of the Annapolis Valley."

Her husband never became rich. He entered politics and was elected County Sheriff. He was a respected figure in the community and was immensely proud of his three sons, one of whom, Charles, was to make the name of Burgess a household word.

Charles Burgess, like many other Maritimers, remained closely attached to his Nova Scotia roots. As a child, he accompanied his mother on trips back to her home. Everywhere the boy looked he would see people making things, doing things, and on their own, figuring out the answers to all sorts of problems. It is tempting to surmise that this heritage—of a sturdy independence—may be what laid the groundwork for the creative thinking which led to his many inventions and his success in life.

Windsor's Unsung Inventor

Most of us in this country are quite convinced that we are not an inventive people. Fixed firmly in the mind of every Canadian child is the belief that, when it comes to technology, we're just not in it and must look elsewhere for the know-how.

Do the facts support that self-effacing image? Or could it be we've underestimated our own native ingenuity. Let us try to redress the balance a little by recalling an inventor who was a Valley boy.

We're all familiar with those white and blue casseroles, pots, and platters known as Corning Ware. Corning Ware is produced by the Corning Glass Company of Corning, New York, famous for their blown glass and their crystal goblets. Corning is to glass what Tiffany is to diamond bracelets. They enjoy an international reputation. A man from Windsor, Nova Scotia, Errol Shand, helped establish that reputation.

Already he had made important advances in electrical engineering with the Westinghouse Electric Company of Pittsburgh. Then, in 1936, he joined the Corning Company as an engineer specializing in glass research.

"We're all familiar with those white and blue casseroles..."

Here, at Corning, Errol Shand became fascinated by the possibilities of weaving tiny glass fibres into a cloth that would be fireproof. By the mid-1940s, Corning was able to market a product that was a milestone in the whole glass-making process—fibreglass. This was to open up a whole new industry, including the manufacture of fibreglass boats.

But fibreglass was only one of the many technical advances pioneered by this young man from Windsor, Nova Scotia. Errol Shand became an expert on the problem of the shattering or fracturing of glass. Out of this work there developed a product that had tremendous resistance to heat and was virtually shatter-proof—the famous Corning Ware.

By this time Errol Shand's reputation as an expert on glass research was well-known in that home of glass making, Czechoslovakia and their glass-making industry invited him to visit their country and advise them on problems they were having.

In 1958, the McGraw-Hill Publishing Company published a book by Errol Shand,

Home of Miss Gwendolyn Shand, Windsor.

Handbook of Glass Engineering. Today this is recognized as the standard text on glass-making.

Errol Shand was more than an inventor; he was a real scientist, both in the field of electrical research and even more in glass research. Yet, this graduate of Acadia University and McGill, although made a Fellow of the American Ceramic Society in 1959 for his "notable contributions to the Ceramic Arts and Industry," is hardly known in his native province.

At the time of his death in 1969, some, even in his own hometown of Windsor, were unaware that he was a brother of the town's distinguished historian, Miss Gwendolyn Shand. At Corning, New York, and in the glass-making capitals of the world, Errol Shand's reputation continues to grow.

Alfred Fuller—And His Brush Company

At the beginning of his career, Alfred C. Fuller, the original Fuller Brush Man, had so little schooling that he hardly knew how to spell. He had grown up on an Annapolis Valley farm, attending the little one-room district school at Welsford. Because his studies were often interrupted so that he could help at home with the chores, or take a hand at apple-picking time, he didn't get too far in *The Royal Reader*.

Alfred Fuller managed to stay in school until he completed grade seven. Because he left school before they started stuffing him full of trigonometry and Latin and Elizabethan literature, he was still able to see things with the direct, unindoctrinated mind of a child—seeing the world as it really is, even to the point of noting that the emperor had no clothes.

Well, the emperor not only had no clothes; he didn't have any clothes-brushes—or any decent ones. So, Alfred Fuller stepped in the door, unpacked his sample case, and proceeded to make the emperor very happy...leaving him a free Handy Brush into the bargain.

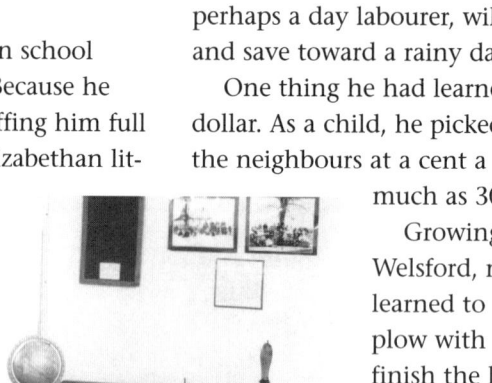

But wait, we're ahead of our story....In later years it puzzled Alfred Fuller. He had never thought of himself as someone likely to succeed in business. In fact, as a teenager, all he could see ahead was the hand-to-mouth existence of a small-time Nova Scotia farmer, or perhaps a day labourer, willing to work hard and save toward a rainy day.

One thing he had learned—the value of a dollar. As a child, he picked strawberries for the neighbours at a cent a quart, making as much as 30 cents a day!

Growing up on the farm in Welsford, near Berwick, he had learned to rise with the sun, plow with a team of oxen, and finish the last chores after dark. He knew how to thin turnips and was good at hoeing potatoes, but so were lots of other boys in the Valley.

His mother and father decided there wasn't much of a future for him on the home farm, so a married sister in Massachusetts wrote back

"...the little one-room district school..."

home and said he was to come down and stay with her... until he found a job.

Soon we find Alfred Fuller in Somerville, Massachusetts, a residential suburb of Boston. The year is 1903, and this is how he saw himself at the time: *The brutal truth is that, at age twenty, I was a country bumpkin, overgrown and awkward, unsophisticated and virtually unschooled. Further, I had been reared in a corner of the earth which offered no springboard to any prospect except the most prosaic rural existence, in an ox-team culture. The seasoning forces of learning and society passed me by. I could scarcely read, could not spell accurately or keep a ledger and was too shy to impress anyone. I had no dreams of greatness to prod me in any direction. In fact, had you been my father or mother, you would surely have put me to work behind an ox-powered stoneboat on a rocky farm and looked for a simple, healthy girl to keep me company.*

But now he was in Boston, looking for work, and he found it on a Boston streetcar, as conductor at $12 for a seven-day week. He kept plugging away at the conductor's job for a year and a half. One morning, the motorman (who earned $15 a week) was late for work. Here was his chance to step up into a

"...there wasn't much of a future for him on the home farm..." Fuller homestead.

motorman's job. He would demonstrate he knew how to drive the streetcar too, so he got at the controls, backed out of the car barn, and managed to derail the car. He was fired on the spot.

Next he got a job as gardener and groom to a wealthy lady in fashionable Arlington. One day, when this lady went riding side-saddle, she found her blue velvet habit covered with white horsehairs. "Look!" she said, "It's ruined. Didn't I tell you to pay particular attention to the currying?"

"Yes, ma'am," said Alfred Fuller. "It looked all right to me."

Grooms were not expected to talk back like that. She handed him the reins, walked to the house, and, a few minutes later, her butler brought him word...he was fired.

His next job was driving an express wagon. He left packages at the wrong addresses, forgot important pickups, and managed to lose a carton or two. So, for the third time, he was fired.

Many years later, he reminisced about those days while addressing the directors of the Bank of Nova Scotia in Halifax. He summed it up this way: "I guess it's quite evident why I became self-employed—I had no choice." The trouble was he just couldn't keep his mind on his work. He wasn't interested and he saw with a child's unblinking discernment that he resented this wage slavery. Nothing he did seemed to satisfy his exacting employers. If only he was on his own. Suppose he sold something from door to door, like...brooms and...brushes....People had to keep their houses clean.

Well, he got such an agency and, at the end of his first day of selling, Alfred Fuller knew right there that, finally, he had found himself—even though he only sold six dollars worth of brushes. But he'd done it at his own speed, in his own way, without a boss standing over him telling him what to do.

He made mistakes, plenty of them, but he figured he could learn from those mistakes. On that first day of selling, he discovered that if he stepped forward when the door was opened, it was always slammed in his face. If he stepped back a pace, which he did in anticipation of another slammed door, it inspired confidence in the housewife.

Even so, the percentage of rejection was high. At this point, Fuller, with his child's clarity of vision, saw why so many salesmen gave up after only a week or so. It was simply discouragement—discouragement at human impoliteness.

It was soon apparent that the reason for those slammed doors was fear. Peddlers, with a long history of sharp trading and shoddy goods, had given the whole business a bad name. Door-to-door salesmen were notorious for fast-talking the gullible housewife into buying a useless gadget, before moving quickly on to the next house.

Something else Fuller discovered: these brushes he was offering for sale were poorly constructed. They weren't made to last, and they weren't the kind of brush the housewife really needed. Several customers explained to him exactly what kind of brush they did want.

That gave him an idea. He went home and tried his hand at making some brushes along the lines that had been suggested. When he went back next week, his customers were very happy to buy them. Without hardly realizing it, Alfred Fuller had established himself as a brush manufacturer—doing it all in the basement of his sister's home in Boston, with a cash outlay of only $65.

Within four years, the Fuller Brush Company was beginning to make itself into a national institution based almost entirely on its founder's first-hand experience in door-to-door selling.

One thing Fuller did not care for was the fast-talking salesman. He didn't talk fast himself—he was much more inclined to be a listener. He always maintained that the product must sell itself. The trick was not to persuade the housewife to buy, but to show her what the brush could do.

But first you had to get inside the door and here you might encounter that most daunting of hazards, for both salesmen and mail carriers—the snarling dog. Fuller warned his men that on no account must a dog be kicked. Its master is probably watching from the window, so the salesman not only loses a sale, but also gains a bad reputation. What he must do is look the animal firmly in the eyes and walk up to the door as though he's a friend of the family, making sure to keep that durable sample kit between himself and the dog. That's how you handle dogs.

Children and babies were even more difficult. An inquisitive baby could reduce the best-packed sample case to rubble while a demonstration was underway. And as for children, they have been known to inform the neighbours that Mamma is entertaining a man...who is not Daddy.

The Fuller Brush Man took all these things in his stride and laughed along with the cartoonists at the many jokes made at his expense. Comedian Fred Allen, on his radio network show, put it this way, "Edison gave us the electric light...Marconi gave us the wireless...and Fuller gave us the brush."

Indeed he had. This largely self-taught man had revolutionized the manufacture of brushes and restored the good name of the door-to-door salesman.

Alfred C. Fuller always insisted he was a very ordinary person, without imagination. He claimed if there'd been intelligence tests in his day, he would have failed them all. Of course, he was anything but ordinary. He was a person of great understanding, with an insight into how to deal with people that amounted almost to genius. It made him into a very wealthy man, the recipient of several honorary degrees, including one from Acadia University. In 1959, he won the Horatio Alger award, while thousands of Fuller Brush Men applauded.

Alfred Fuller's first wife, Evelyn Ells, was the daughter of an Annapolis Valley farmer. His second wife, Mary Primrose Pelton, came from Yarmouth.

During his many years in the United States—he died in Hartford, in 1973, at the age of 88—Alfred Fuller never forgot the countryside where he had spent his boyhood. Each summer he made a trip back to the old homestead at Welsford, in the Annapolis Valley.

In his office, in the Hartford headquarters of the Fuller Brush Company, there hung the symbol of his devotion to his home province—a Nova Scotia flag.

A Visit With Ernest Buckler

Ernest Buckler is a Canadian novelist somewhat in the tradition of E.M. Forster, in that he has established himself as a writer of consequence on a relatively small output. His first novel, *The Mountain and the Valley*, appeared in the early fifties and put him instantly in the first rank of serious Canadian writers.

One chilly November day in 1964, I called in to see Ernest Buckler at his farm, a few miles beyond Bridgetown, going towards Annapolis. I had known him for some years, but he was at one end of the Valley and I am some seventy miles away at the other end so we met only at rare intervals.

He lived in a sturdy comfortable old-time farmhouse, close to the road and sheltered from it by a wide-spreading hardwood tree—a beech, I think it was. The house sits on a slight rise of lawn with a garden that looks down over a protecting enclosure of barns and wagon sheds and linters to the dykelands, stretching away to the Annapolis River. Now the barns were empty, as writing absorbed most of Buckler's energies. He kept no cattle himself, the fields being rented to a neighbour for hay and pasturage. Yet he remained on the farm, in a community largely given to farming, which he called "a good free way of life."

Inside the house, in a spacious kitchen, he invited me to sit beside the kitchen stove, where he did much of his writing, working with a pen or pencil on legal-sized sheets of lined paper held in a clip-board and balanced on his knee. He handed me a few sheets of what he had just been working on. I did not realise at the time that he was giving me a preview of the final chapters of the book that may well be called his masterpiece. He called *Oxbells and Fireflies* a memoir. It is, in fact, his recollections of what life was like in rural Nova Scotia at the end of the nineteenth century.

There seem to me to be two ways one can enjoy a

"He lived in a sturdy comfortable old-time farmhouse..."

book. You can relish what it has to say, or the way it says it. The latter is called style, and Buckler was a master of style, of the calling up of a picture, of a feeling, with just the right words. With his first novel Buckler had established himself as one of our most distinguished authors, with a style all his own. In *Oxbells and Fireflies* he went beyond the merely compelling word—he became a poet.

In his first novel, *The Mountain and the Valley*, the rural background was glimpsed somberly, through the penumbra of a tragedy. But, in this later book, the Nova Scotia farm community becomes itself the protagonist, in an eloquent and moving testament to a time now gone. It was a time when we had time—time to savour the world around, from the smell of spun fleece to the sound of the first partridge drumming on a log. It was a secure world, even to the cellar door, *the one door in the house that never frowned, that did the listening for everyone, to the silent sound of fullness below. In bins and jars, and earthenware crocks, and creamers standing in a tub of cool water while their sidegauges of isinglass showed a layer of marigold yellow growing thicker and thicker above the drift-white milk.*

Yes, it was a time of security, when *even the old were not shunted aside. The sound of their lives had been so long a keynote in the family chord that it never ceased to sound.*

It was a world, this almost lost Nova Scotia, where man and wife felt a rallying concern for each other's tasks. Buckler puts it this way:

"...recollections of ...life...in rural Nova Scotia..."

His was the decision when decision must be made; she was royally screened from the rack of doubt by having his fist-mindedness stand between her and all the hard-eyed problems. Once he'd manned a course, whatever it might be, she only had to disciple it. He was her army and she was his flag.

When age, sickness, and trouble came...love might be given an added strength because of these very things. "Love was," he says, "doubled in the one by the hatred of what went against the other."

Now, some will say that there never was such a world here in Nova Scotia...there never were such people. They are wrong—there are such people. I have met them in the remoter parts of the province...in Wreck Cove, in Cape Breton, where a housewife will still brew the stranger a cup of tea at any hour of the day or night.

It is going. It is going fast—but in this book, *Oxbells and Fireflies*, you will still find a time when, if a man got all his potato seed dropped, he found it not unnatural, but even pleasant, to go over and give his friend a hand in dropping his potato seed. It was a part of the tingling fellowship of neighbourliness that once existed in our valley and which has been caught for us on the tip of Ernest Buckler's pen.

[Ernest Buckler, 1908-1984, and Norman Creighton, 1909-1995, were contemporaries with similar outlooks on life. *The Mountain and the Valley* was published in 1952 and *Oxbells and Fireflies* in 1968, four years after the visit described above.]

The Magical Miss Mittens

How is it that some authors can put words together so we turn the pages more and more quickly, wondering what will happen next?

I have been corresponding with a best-selling author of books for children, Lyn Cook, and she has explained to me how she wrote one of her most successful books, The Magical Miss Mittens, which has as its setting the little village of Granville Ferry near Annapolis Royal.

So how is it done? Well, according to Lyn Cook, *the conscious self has little to do with the process. The main idea generally comes as one intuitive flash. Then, all sorts of bits and pieces come bubbling to the surface to unite themselves with the central theme or ideas.* She says, *It is to me as if the whole thing had actually happened in some past time and I am remembering it, piece by piece but not in sequence. When it is all remembered, the pieces fall naturally into place in plot order.*

That sounds easy enough, doesn't it? But perhaps it is not as easy as it sounds. First must come the intuitive flash and in this case it had to do with the nature of time. She asked herself, "What becomes of all the things that have happened?" All the events in our past, our history...do they just disappear, or do they leave an imprint on our invisible world much as a film receives a negative?

Imagine if there was some way to develop that negative! Imagine if one could view what has already taken place, perhaps hundreds of years ago!

Suddenly she saw a young woman, vibrant and with an uncanny beauty, strangely dressed in the garb of another century, living in an old house, a house where the door to every room becomes a magical portal to times past...if one is wearing a certain pair of mittens—mittens which she knits from a

"...one of her most successful books..."

"...the magical Miss Mittens began to take on a life of her own."

great ball of red wool. And so the magical Miss Mittens began to take on a life of her own.

But where, exactly, was this house with its magical doors? Lyn Cook felt deeply that this story belonged beside the sea, rather than in a suburb of Toronto where she lived with her husband and family. It was decided that the family would take their summer vacation in the Maritimes, keeping a lookout for Miss Mittens' enchanted house.

Driving down through New Brunswick, they were captivated by views of hills and sea. Many of the villages offered glimpses of mellow old Loyalist homes, but it was not until they reached the Annapolis Valley and were passing through Granville Ferry that she cried out, "There it is! Stop the car! There's Miss Mittens' house!" The old house stood vacant and still in a sea of grass. They took pictures of it and our author made some hasty sketches—for oil painting is one of her hobbies.

If you'd like to see a picture of this house, you'll find it included in a publication put out by the Heritage Trust of Nova Scotia, called *Seasoned Timbers*. Known locally as the Mills House, it has since been restored by Mr. and Mrs. R. E. Carlson. Mrs. Carlson was the great-granddaughter of the original builder. It is a house with a graceful hanging staircase. Outside, it is rich in Victorian gothic trim. There are small-paned oriel windows, which came to play an important role in the story. After dark, when these windows are ablaze with light, our three young people, through whose eyes the story is told, know that Miss Mittens is beckoning them to engage in another adventure. Sometimes it is with the Vikings arriving in the New World, or Captain Kidd burying his sea chests at Oak Island. Or they find themselves at Runnymede, taking part in the clash with King John that forces him to sign the Magna Carta. Then they are in Africa where soldiers with gleaming spears are rounding them up for transportation on the slave ships...but always...in the nick of time...the red mittens see them safely back home to Miss Mittens' enchanted house.

As you read *The Magical Miss Mittens*, you feel sure that Lyn Cook is a native Maritimer, or that she must have lived at Granville Ferry during the writing of this book. Such is not the case. Aside from that one glimpse of the house and the village, which fired her imagination, she depended, for much of the feeling of the place, on Maritime friends, some of them living in Toronto. This help she gratefully acknowledges. The Rev. W. T. Jefferson, then rector of the Anglican Church at Granville Ferry, supplied a sketch of the village and many legends including, of course, a ghost story. Others, too, furnished background on the local scene. Shirley Elliott, of the Nova Scotia Legislative Library, and two women, one a librarian and the other a teacher, who had come from Annapolis Royal but were now working in Scarborough, Diane Mason and Beverley Payn, all helped to provide telling details.

The illustrations for this book were done by another former Nova Scotian, Mary Davies, who was born and brought up in Truro.

But of course, the writing of those 233 pages was entirely the work of Lyn Cook. Do you know how long it took her? Only two weeks. She says, *When all the information was finally gathered...my enthusiasm was so great the story was bursting to be told. I called my housekeeper, who runs house and family while I write, and has done for all but two of my books....I need her here because, when I write, I want to live the reality of the book completely, as I do for two weeks, writing eight to ten hours a day.*

So, perhaps it's not quite as easy as it sounds. It does take a bit of work, and, oh yes, something else, too, that magical talent for holding children in the spell of make-believe. This is what has allowed Lyn Cook to give us this entrancing fantasy, *The Magical Miss Mittens* with its setting in the old village of Granville Ferry.

[Lyn Cook is the author of many much-loved children's books. Other titles to look for are, *The Bells on Finland Street*, *Samantha's Secret Room*, and *The Secret of Willow Castle*. At present *The Magical Miss Mittens* is out of print but it remains one of Lyn Cook's favourites and she particularly remembers with affection the setting of Granville Ferry.

Like Norman Creighton, Lyn Cook was for several years a contributor to CBC Radio. She is still writing and has recently completed work on a spy novel for children, which is set in Fort Louisbourg.]

A Wartime Ghost Story

Those of us who haunt the second-hand bookstores are soon aware that dealers keep a sharp lookout for Canadiana and especially for books relating to this part of Canada. Very naturally, such books can have personal and special value for their customers. But sometimes, if the book is issued by, say, a New York publishing house, its Maritime origin may pass unrecognized. It is not generally known that one of the most revered names in American literature, Willa Cather, spent her summers in a little cottage on Grand Manan Island where she wrote such novels as *A Lost Lady, Lucy Gayheart,* and *Death Comes for the Archbishop.*

There have been other writers who have come here for inspiration. One of them, who is not famous like Willa Cather, did enjoy a quite amazing success with a story she wrote in Weymouth, Nova Scotia. Some of you may remember the story, *The Ghost and Mrs. Muir.* It came out first as a novel, a condensed version appearing in the *Ladies Home Journal,* and then it was picked up by Hollywood and made into a movie, starring Rex Harrison and Gene Tierney.

Some years later, it was turned into a television serial which ran for a season or two on the CBC. It was a lighthearted story about a young widow and her family who find them-

"Her son... was able to attend Kings Collegiate..."

selves sharing their seaside home with the ghost of a certain Captain Gregg, who has his own rough and ready seafaring ideas of fun.

On the dust jacket of *The Ghost and Mrs. Muir*, the author's name is given as R.A. Dick. This is a pen name to hide the identity of Mrs. Josephine Leslie, who was Joyce Leslie to her Nova Scotian friends. She was an English girl who, with her two children, spent the war years in Weymouth and Windsor.

At the commencement of the war, she and the children accompanied her husband to South Africa, where he had been posted. While there, Mrs. Leslie contracted malaria and on the advice of her doctor returned to England. There she met some friends from Atlantic Canada who urged her to come out with them to Nova Scotia. This was in 1943.

She settled in Windsor. The town offered her children the advantages of two well-known private schools. Her son, aged 12, was able to attend Kings Collegiate and her daughter, aged 10, was enrolled at Edgehill.

For the children it was an adventure—new sights, new companions, and a new way of liv-

"...her daughter...was enrolled at Edgehill."

ing. It was all quite exciting and overlaid with the hectic urgency of those wartime years. Windsor had become an embarkation camp and the streets echoed to the heavy tread of army boots. To Mrs. Leslie, the sound was only a reminder of the seven thousand miles of wartime uncertainty that separated her from her husband.

She has been described to me as a person with a naturally cheerful outlook on life. But in 1943, there were times when it was difficult to go on being cheerful. Windsor friends entertained bravely with tea and scones. Spirits were buoyed up over a rubber of bridge, but more and more the hours dragged. To distract her thoughts, she began writing.

The school year concluded and Joyce Leslie accepted an invitation to join some friends in Weymouth, not far from Digby. Here, she and the children spent the summer vacation months. In Weymouth, imagination quickened; the dim outline of a character, an old seadog, struck her fancy. Veiled in the foggy enchantment of St. Marys Bay, *The Ghost and*

Mrs. Muir began to take shape.

She found something else in Weymouth: a wharf that had once been a busy loading dock for lumber boats, but now lay almost abandoned—the old Campbell wharf. It was a perfect retreat for the writer.

Out on the end of the wharf stood a little building that had once housed the donkey engine, used in operating the winch when loading lumber. On windy days, the little donkey engine house provided her with an office. On fine days, she sat out on the end of the wharf on a campstool filling page after page of a copybook. Gradually the story developed until it took the proportions of a novel.

After the novel had been published and became a successful movie starring Rex Harrison, a rumour sprang up among her friends. By then she had returned to England, but it was said that, because of her inexperience, she had sold her work for a lump sum to an American publisher and did not share in the sale to Hollywood.

"It was a perfect retreat for the writer."

A similar rumour had for years circulated about the publication of *Anne of Green Gables* which claimed that L. M. Montgomery had sold *Anne* outright to a Boston publisher for $500 and never received any royalties. Such was not the case; Lucy Maud's correspondence shows that she did in fact receive royalties on her famous book.

To verify the facts about *The Ghost and Mrs. Muir*, I wrote to Mrs. Leslie, now living in a little village near Dover, England, asking if the rumour was true. In her reply, she says that the facts "seem to have been quite misunderstood." She did indeed receive her ten percent royalties on the novel along with a satisfactory sum from Twentieth Century Fox for the film and broadcasting rights.

So it turns out there was a happy ending for our wartime guest from England—and the ghost that had its origin in the little village of Weymouth.

Coastal Spring

The bright pour of north wind
Comes from a headland
Where sloped hills of indigo
Are staked with close trees
And anchored by low fields.

Poised gulls,
Crossing the steep sky,
Are drawing lines,
Like curving roads of summer.
Sun-tipped waves
Flow nakedly
Upon the ice-marbled shore.

There are dark-feathered squalls
On a flat sea;
There are green shadows under boats;
There is the flip of silver-flashing oars
Tapping at my heart.

The wide expanse of rippled blue
Is wreathing springward
While, on the glistening horizon,
A little ship
Lies free to the clear sky
Of another year!

Alan Creighton

Fountain of Youth

Tens of thousands of Maritimers have studied Chemistry from a textbook called the *Dominion High School Chemistry*, written by Bigelow and Morehouse.

Used in Saskatchewan, New Brunswick, Prince Edward Island, and Nova Scotia into the 1960s, it had a run of some 35 years—very successful for a textbook. One of the authors, the late Dr. Harold E. Bigelow, was Professor of Chemistry at Mount Allison. His co-author in this widely used textbook was Dr. Fred Morehouse, now [1970] retired and living in Sandy Cove, out on Digby Neck. Although this textbook explained the basic facts of chemistry, such things as the formula for water being H_2O, I don't believe Dr. Morehouse included the formula for a very special kind of water they have in Sandy Cove—a water that quickens the spirit to think young and stay young.

Dr. Morehouse has been thinking young ever since he was a boy growing up in Sandy Cove. All through his career he had to do with young people. For many years he was Supervisor of Schools for the city of Halifax.

Now that he's retired he still likes keeping in touch with the younger generation and listening to their problems. And that's rather remarkable, because next month, in November, [1970] Dr. Morehouse will celebrate his ninetieth birthday.

Now you don't get to be ninety, and remain vigorous and mentally alert as Dr. Morehouse has done, without some secret formula. And I think I discovered Dr. Morehouse's secret last summer while on a visit to Sandy Cove.

Before I reveal this secret, I must tell you something about Dr. Morehouse's great grandfather, John Morehouse, Esquire, Loyalist. He was the first man to settle in Sandy Cove, in 1783; yet only three generations later we have the great grandson of John Morehouse still living in Sandy Cove. Somehow, the people of Sandy Cove manage to get in a lot more mileage than most of us. How do they do it?

The answer to this lies in understanding why John Morehouse chose Sandy Cove as a good place to live.

Like hundreds of other Loyalist émigrés from New York, John Morehouse and his three brothers had sailed down to Nova Scotia with Admiral Sir Robert Digby, who commanded a flotilla of British warships. They came ashore

A view of the cove from an old woodcut.

in Annapolis Basin, at a place that is now the town of Digby, named in honour of the Admiral.

Some did not stay in the town; they wanted to push on further. One Morehouse brother secured passage across the Bay of Fundy. He made his way up the Saint John River and settled in the Keswick Valley, near Fredericton.

Another brother obtained a grant of land at Gulliver's Cove and later moved to Granville Ferry. A third brother finally settled in what is today Centreville, along Digby Neck.

Let us follow the fourth brother, John Morehouse, as he sets out through the woods with his wife and child and his wife's father, looking for a likely spot to build a log cabin. Following Indian paths through the virgin forest, they cut across to the head of St. Marys Bay, then down the shore for some twenty miles on Digby Neck.

Within a mile or so of the present village of Sandy Cove they came on a waterfall. It is there to this day, cascading down over a sheer drop of some fifty feet into a pool below, then finding its way through moss-covered boulders and forest ferns and bracken out onto the beach of St. Marys Bay—a perfect gem of a waterfall. They must have paused here and knelt down for a drink. It seemed like a good place to stop to build a log cabin, which they did, close to the beach—the foundation stones are still there.

What John Morehouse did not realize was that this was no ordinary camping ground; that what he had discovered here in this crystal-clear waterfall was of far greater value than the property he had been forced to leave in the State of New York. In fact he had come very close to the Fountain of Youth.

Otherwise, how can we explain the longevity of the Morehouse family and the even more obvious fact that Sandy Cove itself seems forever preoccupied with anything that has to do with young people?

There are the summer camps, for example. Generations of boys and girls have come here from New Brunswick and Prince Edward Island and Nova Scotia to spend their summers in Sandy Cove, the girls at Camp Arcady on St. Marys Bay, the boys at Camp Champlain on the Bay of Fundy side of this rambling little village that sits astride Digby Neck, with one foot in St. Marys Bay and the other in the Bay of Fundy.

Not only does Sandy Cove go in for summer camps; they have a library designed especially for those who are young at heart.

It was started in 1936 and today comprises some five thousand volumes, including autographed presentation copies from famous authors who have visited Sandy Cove. Some of them lived here and every one of the authors who spent their summers in Sandy Cove wrote stories for children. Now that is interesting. Do you suppose they'd had a drink from the waterfall?

I was shown through this community library by Mrs. Emden Morehouse, the librarian. It took the people of Sandy Cove five years to gather together enough money to put up a building. Not one book in this library was bought; every volume has been donated, and they've built up a most unusual collection, with special emphasis on children's books.

Alice Dalgleish, an editor of *Parents* magazine and one of America's most successful authors of children's books, spent her summers here for many years. Several of her books are built around stories she heard from people who lived in the Cove—such books as *The Blue Teapot* and *Relief's Rocker* which she calls, "A story of Sandy Cove and the Sea."

Another American author, Julia L. Sauer, spent her summers at nearby Little River, and one of the stories she heard there gave her the inspiration for her charming fantasy *Fog Magic*, the story of a little Nova Scotian girl whose love of the fog brought her happy adventures in a village lost for a hundred years.

Mrs. Morehouse enjoys going over to the library each Tuesday and Friday afternoon, from three to five. It keeps her in touch with the young people.

This past summer she had the pleasure of showing a very youthful visitor through the library—someone who helped make the world of the twenties and thirties a cheerful place to live in—Beatrice Lillie, Canada's famous star of musical comedy, who has given command performances before the last three reigning monarchs. She is now Lady Peel. At age 72, Lady Peel is still ready to climb mountains, and when she saw Mount Shubel, a rocky knoll rising some three hundred feet to overlook the Bay of Fundy, she couldn't resist climbing to the top. It took her just 14 minutes.

Lady Peel (or Beatrice Lillie, as her admirers like to remember her) is one of these fortunate people who never seem to age. Her comment on Sandy Cove: "I love it very much." She intends returning. And next time, she may perhaps try a drink from that waterfall. Just to make sure.

[The Sandy Cove Library is open during summer months for the enjoyment of residents and visitors. It is staffed by volunteers. Mrs. Emden Morehouse, now 94, is living in Halifax.]

MI'KMAQ MEDICINES

Near a mossy spring, in a pasture close to where I live, grows the sweet grass the Mi'kmaq weave into their baskets—or used to. They used to come in the fall and gather it, but not any more. For some years now they have not come. I wonder why?

Sweet grass, you know, has magical powers. It is not like ordinary grass. It gives off a scent that is more precious than all the perfumes of Araby. Place some in a room and it will keep sickness away.

Would you like some sweet grass? If you insist on going without it, naturally you will get lumbago. And what do you do for lumbago? Boil some roots of the hackmatack and drink the liquid. That will cure you.

Without sweet grass in the room, you are going to get a sore throat. So chew some bark of the alder. If you should, heaven help you, come down with cholera, do try some ground juniper.

For the cracked skin which we call salt *rheum*, boil the roots of the rock fern down to a jelly and apply it as a salve. Gold-root, chewed raw, cures chapped or cut lips, and the buttercup is a good medicine for almost anything if picked after one returns from church service on Saint Anne's Day—but not if gathered on other days.

Our medical colleges have made no serious attempt to assess, to test and scientifically analyse these preparations. However, when science can provide us with a medicine as potent as thalidomide, such remedies as hemlock bark and sassafras tea must seem too trifling to bother with.

The Mi'kmaq themselves have grown skeptical. Their young people are quick to run to the doctor for a shot of penicillin and to the drugstore for aspirin, so of course, they are just about as sick as the rest of us. But a few still

"...a spring tonic...a little packet of roots and herbs..."

hold fast to the old ways. One of these is my old friend Peter Michael.

[In 1964] Peter is 94. Most of those 94 years he has spent travelling, first as a guide around Lake Rossignol. Later, when he tired of deer-hunting, he became an ambassador of goodwill for his people, travelling the highways on foot, going from house to house, carrying with him a spring tonic: a cheery greeting, a little packet of roots and herbs and a very large tolerance for his fellow man.

Peter is one of the last of the old guard. He can remember the flashing paddle, a singing bowstring, and wigwams fashioned of birch bark, not tar paper. His knowledge of medicine he inherited from his father-in-law, Lone Cloud, who was in his time a chief of the Mi'kmaq people and a famous medicine man.

I once saw Lone Cloud, in the Halifax public market, where he stood behind a stall, dispensing his roots and herbs. A very old man with a fabulously wrinkled face, he carried himself with royal dignity and his long white hair rested on his shoulders in two braids. From Lone Cloud, Peter learned which berries were poisonous, which roots and barks life-

"...a tramp with Peter through the woods."

giving. Nature was the source of both contentment and misfortune; one must be observant and learn how to live with her.

I remember once going for a tramp with Peter through the woods. He noticed so many things I passed by without even seeing—tracks of animals, a hornet's nest built high on a branch, sign of a hard winter with much snow. He pointed out how the tops of the pine trees were bent by the wind towards the northwest. This he used as a compass to direct him in the deep forest.

Then there were the plants and barks he gathered for his medicines—princess pine and black cherry bark, wild turnip, juniper gum, and bark of staghorn sumach which is good for sore throats.

We returned home and warmed ourselves beside the kitchen stove. As Peter settled back in the rocking chair, I asked him what he thought about the people of these Maritime provinces, of the many hundreds of men and women he had met in his travels. What were they like?

"Good people," he said, "friendly people...but many of them very unhappy. They cannot seem to enjoy things." He paused, his eyes seeming to observe the human scene with kindly detachment. "They're always trying so hard," he said. "They can't seem to stop. I think that is why so many of them tell me that they are sick." He shook his head sadly, his face a wrinkled mask of patient resignation.

Peter is still able to get around—taking the Digby boat over to Saint John to visit some friends on the reservation at Big Cove, then returning to the home of his daughter in Middleton. At 94, he is still on the move. That medicine of his must have something in it. But you know, I think the best medicine of all has been Peter Michael himself. A tap on the door, a cheerful smile, a gracious bow....It was as if he truly enjoyed meeting you—and I am sure he did.

WHOSE LAKE?

The open gusts of wind that hiss and run
Across the lake—concealing my leaden track—
Whirl clouds of twinkling mist against the sun.
An Indian with baskets upon his back
Is dim behind the snow the gusts upraise,
Surrounding him within a golden haze.

Who owns this lake? The Indian or I?
That rabbit skipping blithely along a cove?
Or is this white expanse beneath raw sky,
With zigzag spruce indenting a shore of mauve,
For winds alone, through centuries of play,
To laugh upon, to weep—and die away?

Alan Creighton

Pioneer Pollution Fighter

When DDT was being pushed by scientists as a cure-all for the problem of insect pests, the Department of Agriculture, in both the United States and Canada, gave the newly introduced insecticide their blessing. The public was ignorant of the fact that there might be grave objections to its use.

Back in the early 1950s, those who took a biological approach to insect control were being told to pack up and go home. They had outlived their time. The answer to all these insect pests: chemistry—a new wonder-poison, DDT.

At that time, there were very few entomologists with guts enough to stand up at a meeting of scientists and say they were from Missouri—that this stuff needed to be carefully watched, and perhaps banned. That was to come later, much later. In Canada, even a partial ban on DDT took years to negotiate.

Contributing very materially to that ban was the determination of one man who was not afraid to stand up and speak his mind, Dr. Allison D. Pickett. For many years he was head

"Working...with the apple growers of the Annapolis Valley..."

of the Department of Agriculture's Entomology Laboratory in Kentville, Nova Scotia, in the heart of the Annapolis Valley.

Working in close co-operation with the apple growers of the Annapolis Valley, Dr. Pickett devised a spray programme which eliminated, or greatly reduced, the use of such pesticides as DDT, while at the same time encouraging the pests' natural enemies—the predators and parasitic species—which are present in every apple orchard. Annapolis Valley apple growers, eighty to ninety percent of them, followed that spray programme for many years.

Rachel Carson, in her spine-chilling bestseller, *Silent Spring*, paid high tribute to the Annapolis Valley apple growers, and cited Dr. Pickett as a "pioneer in the field of working out a sane method of insect control."

A few years later, Dr. Pickett's expertise was drawn on by the chocolate manufacturers of

"...apple growers...followed that spray programme..."

England. In West Africa, insect problems had been developing among the cocoa beans, source of the chocolate makers' raw material. Dr. Pickett was asked to spend three years in West Africa, tracking down the trouble and working out a spray programme.

As a world authority and consultant on the control of insects, Dr. Pickett felt that what was needed was more public control over our agricultural practices and, in particular, over the pesticide industry. He felt that it was too dangerous a thing to be left in the hands of private industry. Publicly supported research would promote the development of more selective insecticides.

In the meantime, the Annapolis Valley apple growers continued their policy of going easy on the new pesticides, realizing that sometimes the new is not nearly as good as the old. Dr. Allison D. Pickett served as an example to many younger scientists of how they should stand up and speak their minds even when opposed by government or "big business."

[Dr. Allison Picket was born on January 14, 1900, in Lower Kars, New Brunswick. He was a man ahead of his time. It was to be many years before he would be recognized as a forerunner of today's proponents of environmentally friendly products...and the debate continues. Dr. Pickett died on September 18, 1991.]

The Bird Woman of Nova Scotia

Nova Scotia is a great nesting place for birds. Every spring they arrive here from the south; the barn swallows from Chile and Argentina, the yellow warblers from Brazil and Peru, the chimney swifts from Central America, and the hummingbirds from Florida and Mexico.

They stay here during the summer months to raise their young. Then, in September, the flocks begin to gather in preparation for the long flight south. They flock together in thousands in the southern part of the province, waiting for a favourable wind.

Nova Scotia is almost an island; between it and the rest of the continent lies the Bay of Fundy, one of the world's roughest bodies of salt water. It is a flight of some seventy miles across this water to the State of Maine. From here the birds continue on down the coast until they reach their winter quarters. That flight is always a test. Every year some birds get left behind. They are too old or ill to make the journey, or maybe they have injured a wing.

"Inside the house... are housed the winter boarders..."
Louise Daley's Digby home.

These birds that are left behind do not stand a chance. They are not hardy enough to come through our Canadian winter. They would be frozen to death by Christmas. But for all that, some of them do manage to survive, thanks to the vigilance and dedication of a retired public health nurse, Miss Louise Daley, whose hobby is looking after stray migratory birds and seeing them through the winter.

I was in Digby one October when the rescue operation was underway. It is really very simple. A bird cage baited with food is set up in an apple tree, or in the honeysuckle bushes, and a string is attached so that the door can be tripped and closed at a distance, once the bird has stepped inside.

Of course, one's garden must be such as to attract birds, with trees of every kind, including evergreens and shrubs that produce seeds or berries suitable as wild bird food. Miss

Daley's advice is not to be too fussy, but, as she says, "Let it go brambly."

I am sure the birds must be very familiar with that wild and tangled garden of Miss Louise Daley. It is filled with trees, shrubs, rose bushes, and generous paths that wind their way over to the neighbours. It spans the distance between two streets, lying on the steep slope that overlooks the Digby waterfront and the Annapolis Basin.

The birds for generations have known the old, rambling house as a landmark. It has been there, sitting high above the street, for over 150 years, built of hand-hewn beams put together with wooden pegs, split boards (some of them almost two feet wide), and plaster made from clam shells.

Inside the house, in a spacious kitchen, are housed the winter boarders. Their home is a specially constructed enclosure that reaches from floor to ceiling, almost like a high-rise apartment for birds, except that it is all one big cage. It is furnished with a spruce tree and boughs of juniper, with moss underfoot, wall to wall. There are various choices of food: grapes, highly prized by the Baltimore orioles; canary seed mixed with hard-boiled eggs; and, as a special treat once or twice a week, some Canadian holly berries. Miss Daley gathers these wild holly berries in the fall and stores them in the freezer.

Some of the birds are brought to her by children—such as a bird that had been mauled by a cat and saved, at the last moment, by some indignant little boy or girl who snatched it from the jaws of eternity. Most of them, however, have been caught in the outdoor trap.

In the warmth of Miss Daley's kitchen they flit about and sing all winter long. There are white orioles and cedar waxwings, purple finches, juncos, a hermit thrush, and a robin with a broken leg.

Some of these birds become so tame that they refuse to leave in the spring. One junco with an injured leg had to have the limb amputated. He stayed on with Miss Daley, hopping around on one leg, for nine and a half years. But most will be ready to fend for themselves as soon as the warm weather comes. When the apple trees are in bloom, on the first Sunday in June, Miss Daley will unlatch the cage and open the door of her kitchen out into her garden.

The birds will take off like arrows, soaring down over Digby town with the gulls. They are off to Smiths Cove or Briar Island, looking for their brothers and sisters and cousins—or, perhaps, their mate—just returned from the south.

[Louise Daley died on December 1, 1980. She was a wonderful friend to many people. She was interested in all nature, especially birds and flowers and had a regular nature column, for many years, in the *Digby Courier*.]

The Lightning Slingers

He sat there under a circle of light, wearing a green eye-shade and black arm protectors, his ear cocked to the resonator, his fingers poised over a brass key. As the messages came tumbling in, he wrote them out with pen and ink, dipping his pen quickly into the ink-stand to keep up with the words clacking in over the wire.

If you were a boy hanging about the train station or the telegraph office, you gazed in wonder at the mysterious clacking key and the man who sat there understanding it all. In your eyes there was awe, close to idolatry, and there was the hope that he might ask you to deliver a telegram. You might even get a tip of five cents.

The key clicked, the resonator answered, the semaphore was raised to flag down train number 239 as she came rumbling through on her way into the city. Everyone on board is safe while the operator sits there, his fingertip articulating the current in the electromagnetic coil, creating the dots and dashes of his secret language—the Morse code.

Lightning slingers, they called them, or code jugglers, or brass pounders, and today [1964] there are very few of them left. The last commercial telegraph office in the Maritimes still using the Morse code is in my hometown of Hantsport. Dan Saunders is the agent and operator.

The other day I called in to the office to send a message, and stayed to watch Dan send it. The telegraph key he uses is almost exactly the same as the simple equipment used by Samuel Morse, the inventor of the telegraph, on that history-making day in 1844 when he spelled out the most famous telegraph ever sent: the first telegraph—words from the Book of Numbers, chapter 23, "What hath God wrought!" Transmitted by wire between Washington and Baltimore, this was the telegram which could be said to have ushered in the headlong pace of modern times.

America stood on the brink of self-discovery. The pulse of commerce throbbed across a network of wires that soon reached up the eastern seaboard as far as Saint John, NB. This line was supplemented for a brief year, in 1849, by a pony express which dashed back and forth, up and down Nova Scotia's Annapolis Valley between Halifax and Digby, carrying the latest news packet to reach port. It was taken across the Bay of Fundy to Saint John, and then forwarded to New York by telegraph. In 1850, the telegraph was pushed through to Halifax. Soon the wires were spreading out, along the railway lines and into

"...the telegraph office at Hantsport ...[station]"

the farthest reaches of the province. As little as sixty years ago, the only communication between Dartmouth and Sheet Harbour was by telegraph.

And so it continued for many years. The telegraph office was the lifeline to the great bustling outside world. So intimate was its relation to each little town that the agents and operators adhered to a code of ethics, in its own way as strict as that of doctors or priests. The contents of a telegram could not be revealed to a third party without the authority of a court order. The operator could not even say yes or no if someone should say to him, "Did so and so send a telegram?" He was forbidden to accept messages that might be construed as participating in gambling or crime.

In each community, the telegraph operator was recognised as a man who walked a little apart from his fellows, like the doctor and priest, for he carried the burden of many family secrets. Hurry-up money wired to some ne'er-do-well son who was always in trouble, news of sudden marriages that were not always happy ones, stock quotations that spelled financial ruin, the short, clipped desperate understatements of humans caught in a web of necessity....It all flowed back and forth through the flashing, clicking relays.

We have already dropped in to the telegraph office at Hantsport and listened to the tapping key of its agent and operator, Dan Saunders. Let's go back a few years now and see what started him off in this business.

Back in the 1920s, to be a messenger boy for the telegraph office was to earn the envy of every boy in town. You supplied your own bicycle, but the company fitted you out with a smart khaki uniform. Dan Saunders was 15 when he got the job of messenger boy for Western Union, at Antigonish.

He was soon learning the Morse code. When the line was quiet, he sat at the key, practising. Another messenger boy, in Amherst, was also learning telegraphy, and whenever they got a chance, the two of them would try their hand at the key, talking back and forth to each other. (The boy in Amherst went on to become inspector for Canadian National Telegraphs.)

A year later, Dan Saunders began his career as an operator. After a stint at St. Peters in Cape Breton, he came back to the Valley—first to Berwick and then he took over the office in Windsor, Nova Scotia.

Now, this was in the late 20s. At that time, telegraphy had been a well-established profession for sixty years or more. No one dreamed it could ever be otherwise. The word automation had not yet been invented, but something else had been. As the 30s wore on, little by little, a different sound began to be heard in the telegraph office. This was the sound of the teletype, or printer—ironically, the invention of a fellow Nova Scotian, Frederick George Creed, who was born in Mill Village in 1897.

Telegraphers winced at the sound of that machine. Would they quit now, with millions of unemployed walking the streets? Or would they stay on and become the nursemaids of overgrown typewriters? It was a tough decision.

And then, like a thunder clap, came the war, freezing telegraphers to their jobs and six back-breaking years of overtime. Teletype machines were hard to come by, and the telegraph companies were thankful enough to let the old-time lightning slingers take over the additional load. In Halifax, they faced traffic so heavy that Christmas greetings were still being transmitted almost up to Valentine's Day.

"...bored with the scanty dissipations of this sleepy little town."

At Windsor, an embarkation camp had been established close by and Saunders was trying to handle the increased traffic single-handed. Hundreds of men in uniform tramped the streets, growing bored with the scanty dissipations of this sleepy little town. A trip to Halifax, a poker game...that took money. They wanted it, not next week, but right now, today.

They crowded into the telegraph office, grabbing for forms until there were none left, writing their messages on the wall, calling for quick service. Saunders sat there trying to listen to the clicking of the relay while a dozen voices clamoured for his attention. There were appeals to mothers, to sisters, to sweethearts: please send funds...twenty dollars...fifty dollars...a hundred. When the money arrived, an express order had to be made out and a receipt secured. Often a trip had to be made out to the camp, searching for men who, by this time, might have left for overseas.

A second operator was sent to help, then another. A printer was installed, a girl took over the bookkeeping, and still they could not keep up.

In 1941, Saunders was transferred to the main office in Halifax. For three and a half years, he and the 15 other key men worked a seven-day week, their desks piled head high with messages.

Some messages were in code—not the Morse code but a wartime code—carrying top-secret information between the British War Office and General Montgomery who was then conducting his campaign against Rommel. The Germans had cut the cable between Egypt and Gibraltar, so Montgomery was forced to send his wires east to Ceylon, from there to Australia, then through Fanning Island in the Pacific, to Bamfield, BC. From British Columbia, the messages continued by land wire into Halifax, and from Halifax, by cable to England and the British War Office. That was the kind of work that kept those 15 brass pounders busy night and day, in the C.P.R. telegraph office in Halifax.

Shortly after the war, Dan Saunders was transferred to the office in Hantsport, still as a key man. In the years since the war, the printer or teletype almost completely superseded the telegraph key. Train dispatching on most lines is done by telephone. The Dominion Atlantic Railway, however, which runs through the Annapolis Valley, has remained faithful to the invention of Samuel Morse. You can still [in 1964] send and receive telegrams in Morse code at any of the D.A.R. stations maintaining an agent. Only at Hantsport is there such a telegraph office that has its own quarters.

How does it feel to be the last telegraph office using the Morse code? Well, Dan Saunders feels he has been pretty lucky. While others have had to shift over to the printer, he has been able to stick to his key. Sometimes, it is true, he has a touch of telegrapher's wrist, but it passes, and then the key taps on as merrily as ever. He likes to hear the relay clicking. From the sound of it, he can tell who is on the other end of the wire. It might be Reg Casey in Halifax, who handles all the Morse traffic for the Valley; or Mary Walsh, one of the last women telegraphers in Canada; or Dan's brother, Mel, in Windsor. He knows them all by their sound; whether it is heavy and distinct or light and feathery, each communicates his or her own personality. The messages come flashing in over the wires to the receiving relay, where you can actually see the spark, making and breaking, in this secret language of the lightning slingers...that still has the personal touch.

WAY OF LIFE

Way of Life

A cousin of the Creightons has commented, "Norm, you knew us!" Indeed he did. He delighted in our little idiosyncrasies and foibles as he mused about the way of life he found in the small Annapolis Valley towns and as he learned of the way of life enjoyed by people here in years gone by. The essays in this section provide a social history of the Valley from two perspectives.

We have to remember that Norm was airing his views in the 1960s and 70s. In some of the pieces, such as "Every Night at Seven" and "Patches," he is describing the things he saw around him.

In other pieces he is looking back, often with nostalgia, at a way of life in his past or in even earlier times. Norm had a great interest in talking to the older people he met. He was a good listener and wanted to know about their early recollections and to learn about the lives of their grandparents and ancestors. In this way, some of the oral history he recorded reaches back to the end of the nineteenth century.

Since the days of sail, Nova Scotia has not been at the cutting edge of progress, but many people have found that this is the very thing that contributes to the attraction of the province. It is a place which values its past, and the Annapolis Valley in particular is steeped in history. People like Norman Creighton are the ones who have been able to bring life, colour, and humour to what otherwise might be dry statistics.

Sabbath Observance

It is here once again. Another Friday has rolled around, and we can start planning how we'll spend those two glorious days of freedom, Saturday and Sunday.

What a beautiful day it is—Friday, especially Friday afternoon. How did people ever manage to live without Friday afternoon? They did, you know. There was a time when nobody thought too much of Friday afternoon. It was Saturday afternoon they dreamed of. That was back in the early part of this century—about seventy years ago—when we had a six-day working week...six full days of work with only Sunday to look forward to. And even Sunday wasn't all *that* exciting.

Back in those days our weekend diversions were qualified by two sobering words: Sabbath Observance.

Here is one man's reminiscence of what Sunday was once like: *The day was strictly observed in most of the homes; those who shaved had to shave Saturday; boots and shoes must be polished before Sunday; the stable was not to be cleaned out on Sunday, nor eggs gathered, nor any unnecessary work done....We were not allowed to pick berries in summer, or coast in winter, or have any play or sport on Sunday.*

Sabbath Observance was reinforced by many a folk-saying that threatened dire consequences to those who would drive a nail on Sunday or mend a garment. According to some of the old folks, "If you sew a button on a garment on Sunday...you must rip it off on Monday if you don't want to have bad luck." Equally dangerous was cutting your toenails as summed up in this little jingle:

Cut 'em on Monday, you cut 'em for health;
Cut 'em on Tuesday, you cut 'em for wealth;
Cut 'em on Wednesday, you cut 'em for news;
Cut 'em on Thursday, you cut 'em for shoes;
Cut 'em on Saturday, you'll see your true love tomorrow;

> "...nothing was to be done on Sunday."
> St. Andrew's Anglican Church, Hantsport.

Cut 'em on Sunday and you'll have the devil with you all the week.

I like the way that last line ends up without even bothering to rhyme. It really drives home the point that nothing was to be done on Sunday.

There were many who honoured these prohibitions to the letter. Not far from Port Williams, on the south side of Belcher Street, is the Newcombe homestead, which was once the home of Obadiah Newcombe, a much respected farmer who was also Justice of the Peace and Commissioner of Dykes. One morning when Obadiah Newcombe got up to see to the kitchen stove, he found the fire had gone out and they were quite out of fuel. So he hitched the wagon up and went out to the woodlot and brought back a load of firewood. After he'd thrown it off the wagon, he entered the house carrying an armload of wood. He was met by his wife who said, "Obadiah...what are you doing?" "Bringing in some wood." "But don't you realize what day it is....It's Sunday morning!"

Obadiah said not a word. He turned and walked out to the woodpile, loaded the wood back onto the wagon...and hauled it back to the woodlot, just to punish himself for forgetting that this was Sunday.

Among the strictest of these Sabbatarians was the Rev. Mr. Gordon of Annapolis, who, in addition to his congregation in Annapolis Royal, ministered to a little flock of Presbyterians in Bridgetown. They had no church, these Bridgetown Presbyterians, but met wherever they could, often in someone's home. The Rev. Mr. Gordon had a dream that some day they would build a church of their own in Bridgetown, of brick. His little band of followers finally gathered together enough money to purchase bricks to build their church.

The bricks were bought from Mr. Walker, who operated a brick kiln at Carleton's Corner. One Sunday morning, Mr. Gordon was driving back to Annapolis Royal when he noticed smoke coming from Mr. Walker's brick kiln. He drove over to the kiln and demanded to know why they were working on Sunday. Mr. Walker explained to him that in firing brick, the fire had to be kept up continuously—for at least two weeks. They did not dare let the fire go out, even for a day.

"I'm sorry," said Mr. Gordon, "but this is Sunday. You'll have to tell your men to let the fires go out." Mr. Walker nodded thoughtfully and seemed about to comply, then turned and said, "Well, you know, Parson, we want to burn these bricks very carefully. They're the ones you ordered." Poor Mr. Gordon hardly knew what to say. The bricks had already been paid for. He could imagine them being built up into a fine new Presbyterian Church. After a short but painful struggle, he gave the brickyard fires his blessing and proceeded on to Annapolis.

The Family Pew

Tradition is a curious, remarkable, and greatly underestimated force. Tradition is what makes us what we are. For example, we Maritimers have a reputation, and a well-deserved one, for being a friendly people. It is part of our upbringing. For example, there is no law proclaiming that you must offer helpful advice when a summer visitor stops his car to ask for directions. You do these things because that is the way it always has been. Tradition is a mode of behaviour that has been in place for a long while—something you can depend on.

When you go to church on Sunday morning, the chances are that you will search out a certain pew, close to the lectern, or half-way down the aisle, where your family generally sits, where perhaps your parents were accustomed to sit, and your grandparents before them. In other words, that is your family pew. Throughout the Maritimes are churches where families have been using the same pew for generations. So you have this idea of a family pew, not as a prerogative, but simply as a tradition.

There was a day, however, when the family pew was very much a prerogative. In those days, the church—and I am talking now about the Church of England, the established church—sold its pews to the highest bidder who thereupon became the sole owner of that pew for the coming year. It was like buying a season ticket to the theatre. You had a reserved seat, which remained yours just so long as you paid the rent. If you fell behind in your pew rent, you soon found a padlock clapped onto the door of your square box-pew. Then you and your family retired ignomin-

"At St. Mary's Church in Auburn..."

iously to the back of the church. For those who failed to pay their pew rent it was standing room only.

The Church of England was, in those days, a staunch supporter of the Tories, of wealth and privilege, of the establishment, and nowhere is this more clearly evident than in this matter of the family pew.

At Saint Mary's Church in Auburn in the Annapolis Valley, the front pew, directly under the pulpit, was strictly reserved for "Squire" Van Buskirk. There were many "Squire" Van Buskirks throughout the Maritimes. "Those wot had the money sat." What happened to the more indigent members of the congregation is not altogether clear.

There are well-documented accounts of people who were preceded into the church on cold mornings by servants bringing in foot warmers, maybe a brazier holding live coals, rugs, and books. Then, shortly before the service, the "squire" and his family would sail grandly up the aisle, escorted to their box-pew where they would be able to concentrate on their devotions without having to bear the distractions of physical discomforts.

This problem was beginning to trouble

"Those wot had the money sat."

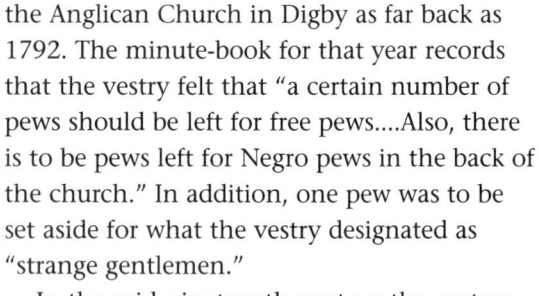

the Anglican Church in Digby as far back as 1792. The minute-book for that year records that the vestry felt that "a certain number of pews should be left for free pews....Also, there is to be pews left for Negro pews in the back of the church." In addition, one pew was to be set aside for what the vestry designated as "strange gentlemen."

In the mid-nineteenth century the custom of renting out pews gradually came to an end. The churches found that the return from this source of income was diminishing. The pews were not selling, so it was decided to make the pews free and have a yearly subscription instead.

This innovation did not meet with the approval of Bishop Inglis of Nova Scotia. He was a man of fine character, a most distinguished divine, but the idea of making the pews free to all comers was more than he could countenance. In a letter to one of the churches in New Brunswick, he wrote:

I never knew an instance before this, in Europe or America, where the pews were thus held in common, and where men, perhaps of the worst character, might come and set themselves down by the most religious and respectable members of the parish. This must ultimately tend to produce disorder

and confusion in the church and check the spirit of true devotion and piety.

When a man has a pew of his own, he can leave his bible and prayer books in that pew when public worship is ended on Sunday, and he will be sure to find them in his pew on the next Sabbath.

The infirmities of age and health require attention to the comfort of warmth, especially in the winter. A man may procure that comfort by lining his pew with some kind of cloth and covering the floor.

It is needless to say that the mode of holding the pews in common must necessarily preclude those with many other conveniences that might be named. What could occasion such an innovation, such a departure from the usage of the Church of England, I am unable to conceive; the greatest disorder must be the consequence, if this mode be continued, when the country becomes populous. In some places it would at this day be ruinous to the church....

Bishop Inglis lived to see a number of churches throw their pews open to the public at large. This was not effected without many regrets and head-shakings. They tell one story about a churchman who was shocked at the social tendencies of his day, and complained that they had taken away *the dear old family pews and made all the pews alike.* He addressed a letter of remonstrance to the bishop, which concluded with these words:

Of course, my Lord, I know that in Heaven we shall all be equal, but I have made up my mind that as long as I live in this world, I will keep myself respectable.

The auctioning off of pews gradually fell into disfavour and was finally given up as church policy. At Saint Paul's in Halifax, all the pews were made free in 1890.

Although each church has its "family pews," recognized as such by right of occupancy, the pews today are open to everyone, to the poor and underprivileged as well as the prosperous. The traditional hand of welcome is extended even to "strange gentlemen."

The Family Bible

It occupied a place of honour on the walnut side-table, resting proudly on the crocheted centrepiece. You couldn't fail to see it when you entered the room; it was so grand, such a massive volume. Bound in imitation leather, it contained maps of the Holy Land, a picture of Moses in the bulrushes, along with Grandma and Grandpa's marriage certificate and temperance pledge. This was the Family Bible.

Grandma used it for pressing flowers. You'll find some faded buttercups in Jeremiah, chapter 15, an autumn leaf still flushed with crimson, in the Song of Solomon.

Grandpa used it for recording the family's vital statistics—the births, the marriages, the deaths. On a Sunday morning, he would sometimes open it to read from the book of Proverbs, "Pride goeth before destruction, and an haughty spirit before a fall. "

Who would have dared suggest that this weighty volume, the authorized King James Version of the Bible, would ever see itself superseded, cast aside, replaced by something more *à la mode*, more with it, more relevant.

"...the Family Bible with the clasps of lacquered brass."

But in 1961 there appeared the New English Bible, a brand new translation, and since then other bibles have beckoned to us from the bookstalls, as entertaining and topical as the latest bestseller. But no matter how sprightly they make the story of Lot's wife or Joseph's coat of many colours, it can't begin to compare with the Family Bible.

In the first place, where is that little piece of crochet Grandma left to press in the 39th chapter of Isaiah? And if we are going to settle the argument about whom Uncle Philip married when he went out to Saskatchewan, there's only one place we'll find the answer. Not in this latest translation—no no, it won't help one bit. It's in the King James Version, the Family Bible with the clasps of lacquered brass. The family history is all there, starting out with Great Grandfather's spidery script and carrying on right up to the present, in the special section between the Book of Malachi and the New Testament.

These Family Bibles are very common throughout the Maritimes. Almost every family possesses a Family Bible somewhere—back in the old homestead, or in a trunk up in the attic, or, in some cases, displayed in a china cabinet as one of the relics of the family, the one sure link with one's ancestors.

Some are to be found these days in museums. There is the Easson Family Bible, which you will see in the museum in Fort Anne in Annapolis Royal. The entries in this Bible were begun in 1741 and it contains records of the Easson family for over two hundred years.

In Wolfville there is a very old Family Bible, owned by the Bayne family. It is a Breeches Bible, so called because in this translation of the Bible, the word "breeches" is used in a very well-known context, in the third chapter of Genesis where it says, "And the eyes of them both were opened, and they knew that they were naked; and they sewed fig leaves together, and made themselves aprons." In this very early edition of the Bible, the translators, anticipating the modern trend of women's fashions, had Adam and Eve sewing fig leaves together to make themselves breeches!

No books are more highly cherished than the Family Bible—our own Family Bible, containing the old authorized King James Version of the 23rd psalm—along with Grandmother's pressed flowers.

"Grandma used it for pressing flowers."

Joys of Travelling by Rail

We have a railroad in Nova Scotia running through the Annapolis Valley, between Halifax and Yarmouth. One of the oldest railroads in Canada, it started operating about 1880, five years before the Canadian Pacific was completed. It is called the Dominion Atlantic Railway, or D.A.R. for short. I've travelled on the D.A.R. hundreds of times and have found the staff unfailingly courteous, cheerful, and helpful—anxious to see that the travelling public enjoys its trip down through the Valley.

Observe that I am talking about the staff, the personnel on this railroad, the men who, in practical terms, actually run this railroad—the trainmen, the station agents, the ticket sellers, the engineers, the conductors—for them, I have nothing but praise. As long as they stay on the job, I do not see how the authorities could possibly justify discontinuing the Dayliner between Halifax and Yarmouth. You would travel a long way to find the kind of service you get on the D.A.R.

"One of the oldest railroads in Canada…" Kentville Station.

The public, it seems, is beginning to realise that this railroad provides something very special. For the past three days, I have been going to the post office just as the Dayliner was pulling into the station, and, on each day, its two cars were packed with passengers. There did not appear to be one empty seat.

Some say these crowds of people who have recently taken to travelling on the D.A.R. are the result of a new service, introduced a few weeks ago, which includes a lunch counter on the train, licensed to sell beer and wine.

It could, indeed, be one reason. The D.A.R. always used to be famous for its lunch counters at various stations along the way. In the early days of railroading, the train was a lot slower than it is today, so lunch counters and eating places had to be provided at almost every station.

At Digby there used to be a lunch room run by two Miss Vyes who specialized in custard pies, which moved someone to compose a short poem that went like this:
Lunches tempting served by the Misses Vye
And featuring oft' luscious custard pie.
At Aylesford, you stopped long enough to sample the fish patties, featured at a restaurant

"I've travelled on the D.A.R. hundreds of times…"

run by Mrs. Patterson. At Windsor Junction, a stop of twenty minutes allowed you to drop in at the Junction House run by Mrs. Haley, whose speciality was a glass of ale and leg of chicken.

During those twenty minutes at Windsor Junction, there was further entertainment provided by several goats that always seemed to be jumping the fences supposed to keep them at home. At that time, in the 1890s, whenever a train arrived at the station, these animals would vault over the fence, climb aboard the train, and roam through the passenger cars looking for something to eat. Apparently no one objected to their coming aboard. Indeed, the passengers looked forward to it as a welcome diversion.

In those early years, travelling by train was something of an adventure, especially for the very young. From the very beginning, conductors on the D.A.R. have always taken very good care of children travelling alone.

On one occasion, a little girl was put aboard the train at Annapolis and her mother asked Conductor Joe Edwards to watch that she didn't get off at the wrong station. Every time he passed her seat, the child would remind Joe anxiously to be sure to let her know when they reached Auburn. At that time, Auburn was a flag station, and in a moment of forgetfulness, Conductor Edwards allowed the train to pass through without stopping. So he pulled the cord and had the train back up to the station, then hastened to tell the little girl that they had reached her stop. She thanked him, opened her handbag and took out a bottle of pills, explaining that her mother had told her to be sure and take a pill when they reached Auburn.

"Aren't you getting off here?" asked the conductor.

"No, I'm going on to Halifax."

Then there is the story they tell about a mother with a baby who got on at Bridgetown. Soon the baby began to cry...and kept on crying, until the cry developed into a wail. A kind-hearted man who was sitting across the aisle became concerned about the baby and leaned over and asked the mother,

"Is there something wrong, madam? Is the baby not well?"

She confided in him,

"Well, as a matter of fact, I came away without any milk to put in his bottle."

The kind-hearted man waited until the train pulled into the next station. Then he took the baby's bottle, stepped off the train, and climbed a fence into a nearby pasture where a cow was grazing. The train crew, meanwhile, held the train while he milked the cow into the baby's bottle.

That railroad must have been run by some very compassionate people. And I almost think that, even today, the Dayliner would wait until that baby's bottle was full.

[Passenger service from Halifax to Yarmouth ceased in 1990.]

"...*its two cars were packed with passengers.*"

Our Good Friend, the Horse

"...the most helpful, affectionate...animal..."

I understand that horses are, once again, being used in the lumber woods. They seem to know how to pick their way through the forest without causing damage, proving once again, that the horse is the most helpful, affectionate, and most knowing animal under domestication.

Some maintain that the mule or the donkey is more intelligent than the horse, which may be the case, but we must admit it's the horse who has horse sense, not the mule.

Among those who back the horse is my friend Bill Whealan of Kentville. He should know. Bill Whealan has been raising horses and riding them since he was a youngster. Now, [1982] he's past president of the Valley Western Riding Club which draws its members from all over Kings County and throughout the Annapolis Valley for shows and competitions at their horse ring in New Minas. They also plan trail rides through the South Mountain, which are participated in by members ranging in age from five to fifty-five.

Bill Whealan claims that horses have more sense, more animal sagacity, than any other four-footed creature in North America. He cites as proof their ability to find water. Suppose you're out riding through the woods and both horse and rider grow thirsty. There is no sign of water anywhere. Well, just let the horse have the reins, let him find his own way. If there's a brook within two miles, he'll take you to it. It seems that horses can smell water at a great distance.

Not only that, if the water isn't good, if it's stagnant, he won't drink it. He'll snuff at it, snort over it, but unless he's very thirsty indeed, he won't touch it. He knows better.

One breed of horse with exceptional intelligence is the Morgan, a breed that came into New Brunswick from the state of Vermont. Some years ago, a man living in Saint John, who owned one of these Morgan horses, harnessed up his mare, Hattie, to the surrey one morning and drove down to the waterfront to see a friend off on the Digby boat. He went up the gangplank with his friend, to help carry one of the suitcases but he stayed aboard too long. The boat cast off, and there was his horse left standing on the dock. He called back to someone standing on the wharf, "Phone Worden's Stable to send a man down for my horse." They didn't hear him, so Hattie stood there on the dock all day long...without food...without water. No one suspected the horse's owner had been whisked off to Digby, fifty miles across the Bay. But when the Digby boat returned to Saint John that evening, here was Hattie still waiting and neighing happily at the sight of her master standing by the ship's rail.

There is a story of another man, a doctor, who had a very clever horse. When he went about making his house calls, the horse soon learned which houses to stop at. He did not have to be told. He knew all about Mrs. Brown's heartburn and Mr. Tracey's lumbago. But, like any sensible person, this horse grew tired of always having to wait for the doctor while his patients enumerated all their symptoms. He took to moving along the street and browsing on people's lawns. When the doctor came out of the house, horse and carriage were two blocks away. He tried to cure the horse of this habit by purchasing a length of leather strap with a weight attached at one end and a snap on the other. He snapped it to the bridle so the horse was anchored to one spot, so to speak. But the horse figured this one out very easily. He simply took the strap in his mouth, lifted the weight, and carried it along the street to a nice patch of grass and then dropped the weight.

"...horses have...more animal sagacity, than any other four-footed creature..."

The most dramatic horse story I ever heard was one I ran across in Yarmouth some years ago. The man who told it to me had a laconic turn of speech. He did not waste words. This story, which included all manner of exciting things...sex...violence... just about everything, he summed up in these few words: "Neighbour of mine...beat his mother to death with an axe handle....Had a trial but...he got off somehow....Later on...had fight with his wife...threw a lighted lamp at her and...it exploded and killed her....Got thirteen years in Dorchester for that but...served only ten.... After he came home...horse ran away with him and killed him.... Horse knew more than the judge did."

That just shows you how intelligent horses can be.

STOCKYARDS

I saw a man there
With gentle eyes.
He was leading a horse,
Smooth-flanked and glossy.
Behind him the cattle pens
Showed occasional lifted heads
As under the great sky
Of a grazing foothill.

Alan Creighton

The Barber Shop

In most small towns, you may still find a man who enters himself on the voting list as simply barber—not hairstylist, not hairdresser. This man belongs to a dwindling profession, a sort of vestigial remnant of a once noble institution.

The barber shop has fallen on evil days, to the point where many of us have no idea what a barber shop looked like, in the full pride of its masculine monopoly, with its shelves lined with shaving mugs and bottles of spectacularly coloured hair tonics and dandruff cures, while customers lolled off at ease under a Vesuvius of steaming towels.

What has happened to all this glory? Let's see if we can trace our way back to the first seeds of its dissolution. The great war of 1914 to 18 swept away empires, overthrew dynasties, exiled kings and princelings, and toppled that last throne of male supremacy—the barber chair. Women secured the vote! They brought in prohibition to keep their men from hanging around the saloons. Then, to really sober them up, they started shortening their skirts and ended up by cutting off their hair.

Women began pushing their way into barber shops, demanding boyish bobs and marcel waves. Once they got inside, they took over, cleaned it up, threw the spittoon into the back shop, banned the barber shop quartet, and left most barbers completely unnerved and unable to put up any real resistance.

The barber had to start changing the towels! Before the women showed up, there used to be a saying around barber shops: The first customer on Monday morning gets the clean towel for the week. After *she* took the chair, they had to have a clean towel every day.

It is easy to understand why women were longing to get into these barber shops and take over. For years and years they wondered what it was that went on in there. The men always seemed to come out in such a good humour,

"In most small towns, you may still find...a barber..."

"...lather whipped up in the mug."

humming a song and smelling faintly of lilac water and Glover's mange remedy.

What went on, of course, was sheer hedonism—a series of luxurious rites, such a pampering of the flesh, that men today can scarcely believe that there was this temple to male vanity. I've had it described to me by those around town who can still remember. In those days, they offered all manner of flattering amenities such as face refresheners, scalp vibrators, devices for restoring and stimulating the growth of hair, along with shampoos in a bewildering variety—egg shampoos, milk shampoos, medicated tar shampoos….

While preparations for the shampoo were going forward, the hair itself was cut or trimmed, followed by a singe. This was done with a lighted taper. The purpose of singeing the hair ends was to keep in the hair oils. It was believed that the hair was hollow, and, without singeing, the oils would drain out and leave the customer exhausted and unable to face the road. But, this way, he was always kept full of oil and was able to get in a lot of extra mileage.

Following the shampoo, the patron's face was swathed in steaming towels, while the razor was given a final stropping and lather whipped up in the mug. A shave like this, a really close shave, was known in the profession as "three days under the skin."

The whole thing was not complete unless topped off with a massage. This meant further application of hot towels, impregnated with witch-hazel, finishing up with two cooling towels and a rub-down with June Clover Water. It all cost less than a dollar, and you stepped out onto the street tingling with good will and bay rum and trying to remember the latest jokes.

Today, our barber has a sign up over the cash register. It says "No shaving." It does not even bother to add "No shampoos." They have not given a shampoo or a massage for so long that there is hardly a man in town who can remember what it was like. We all have to do our own shaving at home now. All we can get at the barber shop is a haircut, without the singe.

But, right across the street, there is now a Beauty Salon. It's crowded all day long … and there is such a lot of laughing and gabbing going on. I often wonder what it is they do in there. Over the window curtains you can see the rows of them sitting there under the hair dryers, like giant mushrooms, chatting and exchanging the latest gossip.

There are times I almost fancy I hear them singing, and it sounds awfully much like a quartet….

The Ice-box

There are many Canadians living today who have never seen an ice-box. They have no idea that this was the way people kept their food from spoiling, back in the 20s and 30s and even into the 40s.

An ice-box was a chest in which the housewife used to store food, to keep it cool—much like our modern refrigerator, only, instead of electricity, the driving force was simply a block of ice.

You put the ice in a special compartment and this brought the temperature inside the box down close to the freezing point. As the ice melted, the water ran down into a pan under the ice-box which had to be emptied. Every now and then, someone forgot to empty it, and then it overflowed and the water went all over the kitchen floor.

You bought your ice from an ice-man, who came around in a truck once a week and sold you a tremendous block of ice, as much as he could carry in—along with a lot of sawdust,

"An ice-box was a chest..." (sometimes even built-in, so ice could be put in from the porch.)

which he tracked through the house. If the ice was too big to go into the ice-box, you had to take an ice-pick and hack away at it until it was small enough to slide in. All that, mind you, just to keep the milk from going sour.

It is hard to believe people went through such a tedious ritual. My, what they put up with, back in the days before the electric refrigerator and its effortless convenience. How much simpler things are today. It really is a wonderful age we live in.

Of course, when our grandchildren grow up and take over, I suppose they will look back and think us a little old-fashioned. There seems to be something of the scullion in our constant preoccupation with the washing and cleaning that is always going on, and with all these soaps and detergents. Surely they will find some way to keep the housewife from bending over the washing machines she is always fooling with.

And another thing…in the days to come, they will look back on the insane way we hurtled about the countryside in little tin boxes called motor cars (you may still be able to see them in museums) that kept everybody hopping with monthly payments to the finance company. The way they laboured over those machines and hung about the garage waiting for a valve to be tightened, or a spark plug cleaned….They thought they were having fun, when there was this modern new way of getting around the country—using jet propulsion!

It makes one rather squirm, doesn't it, to think of all the condescending things our grandchildren will find to say about us?

But, back to the ice-box. I can't remember it being such a chore, even emptying the pan under the box. I thought it was a pretty

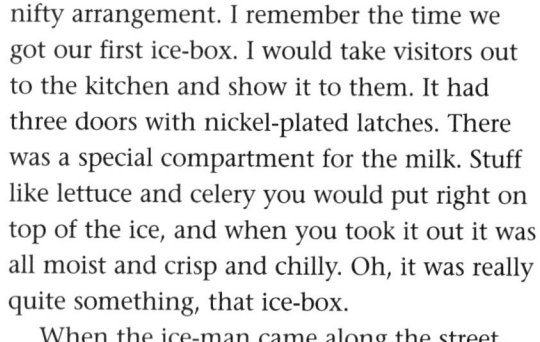

"You put the ice in a special compartment…"

nifty arrangement. I remember the time we got our first ice-box. I would take visitors out to the kitchen and show it to them. It had three doors with nickel-plated latches. There was a special compartment for the milk. Stuff like lettuce and celery you would put right on top of the ice, and when you took it out it was all moist and crisp and chilly. Oh, it was really quite something, that ice-box.

When the ice-man came along the street, he always stopped at our house. There were many houses he did not stop at. Those people didn't have an ice-box. They looked out of their kitchen windows, sipping their sour milk, and watched the man lugging those big shining crystal blocks up our steps for our ice-box. Status-seeking in those days was worth emptying an occasional overflowing pan of water.

Today, we have an electric refrigerator—and the neighbours couldn't care less.

That Brass Spittoon

Let's talk about something that is straightforward, square-shooting, down to earth, and completely antiseptic. Let's talk about chewing tobacco.

I suppose there are people today who have never seen a man chewing tobacco. I have not seen one in years, not since they removed the pot-bellied stove from the waiting room at the train station. At one time the tobacco chewers were all over the place—and so was the tobacco juice. In a high wind, it was a pretty risky business to be walking down Main Street, especially in the vicinity of the hotel, where several men would be sitting out on the front piazza, feet braced against the verandah rail.

Inside the hotel, of course, in the lobby—and this was true of any self-respecting hotel—they strategically placed a massive ornamental cuspidor, so as to draw fire away from the potted rubber plant.

I wonder what happened to all those brass cuspidors? No doubt the collectors are after

"...it was...risky... to be walking...in the vicinity of the hotel..."
Evangeline Hotel, Hantsport.

them. Soon you will see them under glass cases in the museums, a symbol of the less inhibited manhood of our forefathers.

The disappearance of the cuspidor is just another instance of woman's irresistible influence as a consumer. She herself did not have the nerve to take up chewing; so she started making it tough for her husband. She installed an electric range in the kitchen, and that left him completely baffled. He had to swallow his pride, or go out to the back door.

Finally he was driven to resorting to the general store, which became the unofficial club for tobacco chewers. In the middle of the store stood a beehive stove, to supplement the ever-present brass spittoon.

Men were catered to in so many ways. Even the act of purchasing a plug of chewing tobacco afforded him a certain entertainment. The grocer kept the tobacco in a long wooden box. From this he drew forth a bar of fig tobacco, about a foot long, crimped at intervals where it was to be cut. The cutting was done in a special device, like a guillotine. Every store had one, and slicing off a plug to precisely the right size required a judicious eye. It drew an admiring audience of every youngster in the store. By the time you had a fresh plug in your hip pocket, your manhood had been thoroughly established.

Yes, those were the days when men were men, and women spent their time mopping up after them. I think perhaps the whole sentiment and atmosphere of those days, and an intimation of the future, is caught in a little poem I once heard while travelling in the smoking car. It is a mournful little piece, but it has a message.

Within a saddened bedroom, a dying father lay.
His children, in the kitchen, were in gloom that fatal day.
Then the bedroom door did open, and the mother gray with pain
Looked at her weeping children and sang this sad refrain:
"Oh, throw away that brass spittoon, for Dad will chew no more,
And we'll get some new linoleum to lay upon the floor.
For he has gone to heaven to sit upon a throne,
And fine-cut, plug and hard-twist, in heaven, are unknown.
Your father loved his chewing but his aim was very bad,
And when he missed that brass spittoon, it made my heart so sad.
But I won't have to scrub the floor, each blessed working day,
So, children, dry your tears and throw that brass spittoon away."

The Grand-daddy Armchair

When Grand-daddy got married, he furnished the parlour with a cozy assortment of betrothal chairs, love seats, and one especially form-fitting chair which, even in those days, they called "the grand-daddy armchair." In the evenings, he would sit there under a soft pool of light from the kerosene oil lamp, viewing the world through that herald of modern times, the stereoscope.

That was the beginning of it all. From then on, more and more products of the factory crowded into that stuffy little parlour. It was the age of *art nouveau*, the new art, of fumed oak, oxidized hearts, and pictures framed asymmetrically. We were keeping up with the times.

Little by little, the old furniture found itself consigned to the kitchen or hidden away in a cobwebbed recess in the attic. The grand-daddy armchair got put away in the barn loft, under a pile of hay. It was something of a pity because it really was a very comfortable chair. It had been made right here in Nova Scotia by a local craftsman.

The old furniture continued to have a rough time of it until, in the 1920s, dealers in antiques discovered that Nova Scotians set no store by these things—were, in fact, delighted to get rid of them for a five dollar bill. So, every summer, the trucks began coming, gathering up a stuffed-back settee, some Vauxhall plate mirrors, a riband-back Chippendale, along with a grandfather clock or two. Soon, the old furniture found itself back in circulation again—but this time in Boston and New York.

Back in Nova Scotia, they were all agog to get one of those new overstuffed Chesterfields. With one of those in the parlour, there certainly was not room for all this old out-of-date stuff—so let's get rid of some more of it.

"...old furniture found itself consigned to the kitchen..."

"…and soon she uncovered the old grand-daddy armchair."

They kept on getting rid of it, all during the 30s, the 40s, and the 50s. The dealers were so very obliging. They were such nice people...and they always paid cash.

Then, in the 60s, something began to change. Canadians began crowding into the cities, looking for apartments—one-room apartments, or a room and a half. What kind of furniture can you tuck into two small rooms? The overstuffed armchairs were the first casualties, then the Chesterfield had to go. Apartment dwellers were looking about for furniture that did not take up so much room, and they found it in the auction rooms and at the antique dealers. People started taking an interest in finishing furniture and upholstering. Adult education classes were given in how to restore old furniture.

The other day, a girl came home from the city to spend her vacation on the home farm, not far from where I live. She began poking around in the barn loft and soon she uncovered the old grand-daddy armchair. She dragged her treasure into the house.

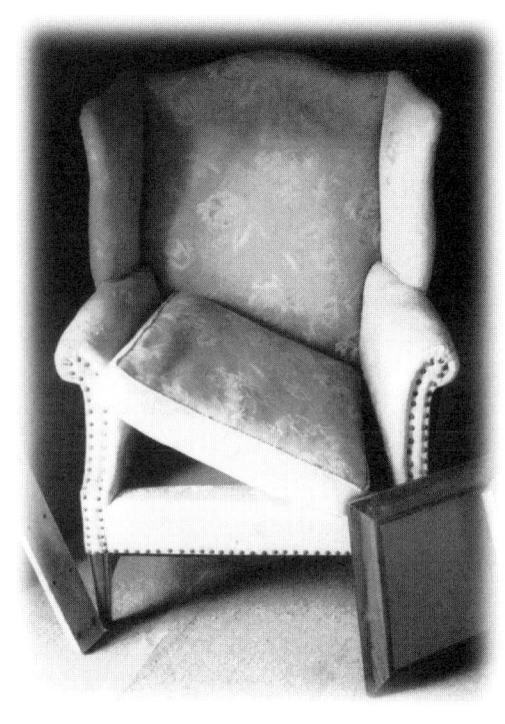

"Look at this," she said to her father.

"That old thing!" her father said, "what do you want with that?"

"I'm going to take it back to my apartment and have it fixed up."

"Oh now, look here," said her father, "if you want some furniture for your apartment, I'll give you some money and you can go out and buy something at the department store—some decent furniture."

She regarded her father for a moment, trying to bridge the generation gap.

"You don't understand. I don't want my apartment to look like a store window. I want it to look a little bit like home. If you don't mind, I'll take the grand-daddy armchair." And, being a thoroughly modern young woman, that is just what she did.

Royal Road to Reading

> "...this little red, linen-covered volume..."

Do you remember the reader you studied when you first went to school? I remember the one I had in grade two. It was called *The Nova Scotia Reader*. On the cover was emblazoned the provincial coat-of-arms. Beneath this heraldic device, were words I shall never forget: "Price 11cents. The T. Eaton Co. Limited, Toronto and Winnipeg." Like hundreds of other school textbooks, it now lies forgotten, heaped up in a dusty corner of some second-hand bookstore.

But, there was a school reader used by an earlier generation that has not been forgotten. It was called *The Royal Reader*. This is a classic among school readers, as well-known in England, where it was first published, as in Canada's Maritime provinces.

People still talk about it. In fact, this little red, linen-covered volume enjoys a certain revival every summer, during the tourist season, when it is sought out in second-hand bookstores by former Maritimers who have heard their parents or grandparents speak of it with chuckling affection.

Now, can you imagine, seventy years from now, any bookstore displaying the readers currently being used in our schools? I can't, and that is not because they are not fun to read. They are charming books which, I am sure, would delight the heart of any child. Just glancing through these brightly-coloured pages, in which laughing boys and girls and romping animals tumble from page to page, makes anyone feel good.

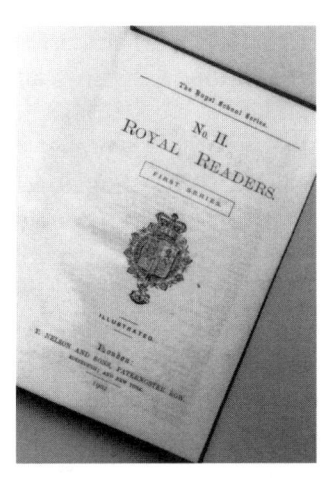

But that is just it. Is it the purpose of a textbook to make you feel good? A bottle of beer makes you feel good. Lots of things make you feel good but they do not necessarily make you *think*. The children of seventy years ago were considered old enough to start thinking once they picked up their *Royal Reader*.

First let us take a look at a reader currently being used in grade one. It is bright and cheerful, full of colour. Here is a story called "The New Book." From it, we get the feeling that books are not so much a source of inspiration or wisdom, or even knowledge, but rather an instrument of fun.

"See this new book!" called Jack. "I found it in the book wagon. Come and look at it."

The children all went to the book wagon.

"This is my new book," said Dick. "I put it in the book wagon for a surprise."

"Miss Hill," called Jack, "Look at the funny school bus in Dick's new book."

Miss Hill came to the book wagon. She looked at the funny bus in Dick's new book.

"I like this book," said Miss Hill. "We can have fun with it. Come to your chairs, children. We will all have fun with the new book now."

All right, that is the new approach. The idea is to have fun. It is spelled out in the titles: "Fun at Home," "Funny Bunny Rabbit," "A Funny Surprise," "Happy Days at the Farm," "A Funny Party." So it goes on, smiles piled on smiles. Everything is bright, new, prosperous and sparkling—one long paean to euphoria.

This grade one reader was prepared by professors of education from the University of Saskatchewan and the University of British Columbia. It was published in Toronto. With such sponsorship, its Canadianism is unassailable, and it may truly reflect the warming abundance of our happy land.

The great weakness in all this, of course, is that it lacks drama. Drama does not exist until someone is in trouble—until they stop having fun.

The authors of *The Royal Reader* had a real zest for drama. Before the scholars had time to unpack their slates, they were plunged into a hair-raising situation, such as the one on page twenty called "The Storm," which depicts, in a sharp etching, a square-rigged ship being pounded to pieces on the rocks. The crew is clinging to the rigging and a lifeboat is trying, desperately, to reach them. I will just give you a few of the more tense moments.

"See, the boat seems to sink in the waves! Down, down it goes. Oh, the poor men!"

"But see, there it is once more! It is on top of a wave....Now it comes near the shore. Pull, men, pull."

It goes on like that for several more paragraphs....It just gets you all worked up. Heartache...tragedy...*The Royal Reader* had the children biting their fingers in suspense as they read this story called "The Last Cross Word."

"Oh," said a little girl, bursting into tears, when she heard of the death of a young friend, "I did not know, when I saw her that it was the last time I should have to speak to Amy!"

The last time they were together, it goes on, she spoke crossly to her friend and those last cross words lie heavily on her heart.

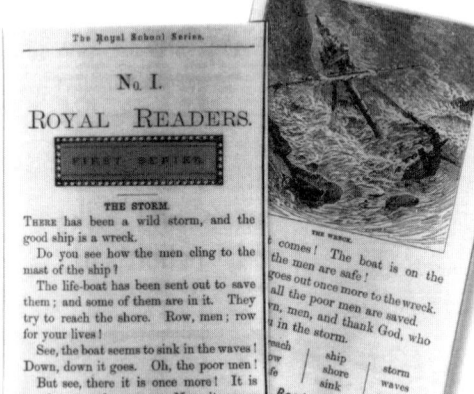

This points out a good rule about kind words. Speak kindly to your father, to your mother, to your brother and sister, to your playmates, to everyone around you, lest it should be the last time you will have to speak to them. Cross words are very sad to think about.

"...the long solitary walk home..."

Now, if this failed to touch their flinty little hearts, they brought on a character known as "the poor old man." Sometimes he is creeping along the street in a big windstorm, and his hat blows off. The boys all laugh and refuse to run after it—but not the good little girl. She runs after it and retrieves it for him. Sometimes he sits under a tree, by the side of the road. His dog is beside him, waiting for the poor old man to share a few morsels from his meagre meal. After we have watched this mournful scene long enough, the author comes forward and says,

"Let us go and ask the old man to come in. Jane will bring him some warm food. Come in, old man, and sit by the fire and rest."

Oh yes, and speaking of Jane, she is the one who had a pet bird in a cage. One day her aunt sent her a box of new toys, and she was so pleased with them that she played with them all day, and the next day, and the next.... Finally, when she tired of the toys, she went to look at her bird. It lay dead in the cage. It had starved to death all because Jane had become so absorbed with her new toys that she had neglected her duty.

From each of these stories, the student of seventy years ago drew a moral. He was left with plenty to think about on the long solitary walk home, through those quiet country lanes. Life was real, life was earnest. In the wings lurked the pinched faces of poverty and starvation, waiting to pluck down those who had not learned the lesson that work is a virtue and idleness the most deadly of sins. Constantly throughout *The Royal Reader,* the student is reminded that he must not waste precious time, nor expect to spend his life in play. The fruits of idleness in childhood are bitter indeed. Fun seems to be unheard of.

However, it is this book, this *Royal Reader,* that is still being sought out in second-hand bookstores, by those whose grandparents remember it fondly.

The Thumbtack Gazette

In this newspaper there are no headlines. It dispenses with editorials. All contributions are welcome—provided you bring four thumbtacks. Otherwise your item would flutter to the sidewalk and end up in the gutter—the way so much journalism does. I am talking, of course, about our town bulletin board.

If you want a glimpse into a little Maritime seaport town, then stop at the corner of William and Main streets, almost directly opposite the hedge of old-fashioned French roses, the ones with the fragrance of cinnamon. My home town is not big enough to support a real newspaper; so, instead, we have

"...all contributions are welcome—provided you bring four thumbtacks."

a town bulletin board. I imagine there is no newspaper in Canada that operates as cheaply as our *Thumbtack Gazette*. Its only overhead is the spreading bough of an elm tree, and its advertising rates are zero, specially in the wintertime.

As for circulation....Well, you would not expect it to circulate very far, when it is anchored to the ground by two stout pieces of timber. But this does not prevent wide dissemination of news. I should say not. Though it stands exposed to wind and rain, the coverage is about perfect. Everybody reads it. You can't help reading it; it's so convenient, being only a step off the sidewalk. In our town there is just one main block, which includes the post office, the United Church, and the volunteer fire department, so you are bound to pass the bulletin board. Maybe you have gone to fetch the mail, or maybe you pass it on your way to the government wharf, to see the schooner *City of New York*. She is the one Admiral Byrd once used on his expedition to the South Pole, and now she's down at our wharf loading lumber. You can hardly do anything in our town without going around the block. We figure it is much simpler to have the public do the circulating.

If anyone started a real newspaper, I am afraid the competition from our bulletin board would be overwhelming. Take now the time, last winter, when little Pamela Brown lost one of her mittens. Now the person who found that mitten did not bother putting an ad in the paper. It wouldn't have done any good if they had because Pamela is not old enough to read, having just graduated from primary class. But, as she came home from school, here was her mitten hung up on the bulletin board—but not too high—just high enough so Pamela could reach up and get it. No newspaper could compete with service like that.

Maybe you are not familiar with a town bulletin board. It works like this. Let's say you have a black Jersey cow; lots of people in our town keep a cow. Well, right now, you are starting to worry about where you'll get enough hay to see her through the winter, for we did not have a very good crop last summer and hay is scarce in Nova Scotia. You could sell the cow but then you would have to buy

"Baby carriage in good condition…"

milk for that kid of yours. He's almost two and very fond of the milk from that black Jersey cow. It is so good for him that he is getting to be the huskiest youngster in the neighbourhood. Look how he pushes his baby carriage around all by himself….No, you could not sell the cow. You just have to find some more hay.

So here is what you do. You sit down and grab a pencil and a piece of paper, and you write in your fairest hand, "Baby carriage in good condition. Will trade for half a ton of upland hay." Then you take the notice uptown along with four thumbtacks and tack it up on the notice board. Did I say upland hay? But then, if anyone offered to trade you half a ton of marsh hay, you might even throw in a dollar or two to boot, along with the baby carriage, because Jersey cows are notoriously fond of marsh hay, the kind we harvest on the salty tidal shores of the Bay of Fundy.

Here is another thing! While you are posting up your notice, several customers from the hardware store cross the street to see what it's all about. While you are chatting with them, you pick up all kinds of information. Did you know that, yesterday, those carpenters who have been repairing the roof of the Baptist church found a wild bees' nest up in the steeple? They got almost two barrels of honey—mind you, not this tame honey either—the wild stuff, drawn from the nectar of fireweed, the real McCoy....

And here's news: Peter, the Mi'kmaq guide is in town today and he says we can expect a cold winter. How does he know? The fur on the muskrat and deer is extra thick this fall, a sure sign of a cold winter. But as to how much snow there'll be, he couldn't say, for so far he hasn't seen a hornet's nest. If you should see a hornet's nest built high off the ground, that means we are in for a heavy snow....These newspapers with their daily weather reports! Around our bulletin board, you can get the whole thing mapped out for six months in advance. We feel anything less than that is hardly worth bothering with.

Are you inclined to mislay newspapers? So am I! There is one great advantage to our town bulletin board. It is always right where you left it; no one ever carries it off. Our Chief of Police would soon run them in if they did. But who would do such a thing? Imagine anyone unfeeling enough to wipe off the top of the kitchen stove with an item like this: "Women's Institute—Meeting on Monday afternoon, to pack baskets for shut-ins. Please bring some of the following flowers for decorating the baskets—native holly, spruce and

"...the hill where you...see our town laid out at your feet."

pine greens, sea lavender, marsh goldenrod." Can't you just see those baskets? What a breath of the Acadian dykelands they will bring to someone who can only sit by the window and watch a seagull soaring high over Main Street, and then winging its way back to the wharf and the river.

Oh, don't read *that* printed notice. It's not supposed to be here. It should have been torn off weeks ago. No, they haven't had dancing at the Community Centre since the last of August. I know it says "Bingo and Band Concert every Wednesday night," but that was during the summer, when our Community Fair Grounds made the long evenings gay with music and laughter, and, after sundown, the coloured lights under the big overhanging trees cast a spell of enchantment on the warm summer nights. There in the pavilion, under the stars, the young folk wore paper hats and danced to the rollicking tunes of an old-time fiddle. How far off it all seems now, now that the changing leaves from the oak trees are drifting down onto the dance pavilion, where men are taking down the coloured lights.

You see, sometimes these notices get left up by mistake....But you can soon tell. The paper

"...the corn-stalks of the kitchen garden..."

begins to turn up at the edges. If the writing is with pen and ink, the ink grows fainter and fainter after each driving rainstorm, so after a while you can hardly make out what it says. Some of the notices are protected by a sheet of cellophane, which tells us the contributor is a careful and thoughtful person—like this one here, "Additions to our school library are solicited. Nature books especially welcome."

Oh, speaking of nature books—this afternoon, I believe, grade three is going for a nature ramble. They always do, every fall. Why yes, here they come now, trooping out onto the sidewalk, two by two, off for a tramp up to the top of the hill where you can stand and see our town laid out at your feet. The oaks and elms are turning colour now, white houses peeping out here and there, spires of churches, the government wharf, with a Norwegian steamer loading bales of pulp for Baltimore. Teacher is pointing out a flock of robins in the rowan trees. There are hundreds of robins gathering for the final feast of the season. Tomorrow all the bright berries will be gone, and so will the robins. The blue jays will be here to take their place, searching the cornstalks of the kitchen gardens for a stray cob of corn, the wind ruffling their top-knots, jaunty, debonair, undaunted by the approach of winter. For downright education, there's nothing that can equal a nature ramble, conducted by one of those pretty schoolteachers. They are all good looking in our town, but they never look so charming as when surrounded by an eager group of boys and girls, swinging along in the autumn sunshine.

I told you that everyone reads our notice board, but not everyone contributes to it. Some have, perhaps, a more literary bent than others, or maybe it is just that they are more daring. You know, it does take a little nerve to push your way in among the bystanders and stick up a notice that says, "Salmon net and motor boat. Bargain—for quick sale." We all know that salmon net you're talking about. We've seen it hanging up to dry down at the wharf. Why are you selling out? You were on the river drifting for salmon and shad all summer. Aren't you figuring to drift next summer? Don't you like drifting on the river for salmon? Maybe you're shipping out on one of the lumber boats....No? It takes courage to face that kind of cross-examination. You know the kind of embarrassing questions people ask....

Sometimes folks will wait till after dark, until there is nobody around, then steal quietly uptown and tack up their item. In some cases this shyness is very understandable. Suppose now you are a girl whose boyfriend has given you a pair of earrings for a birthday present, but you went and lost one of them. Now you are in a jam. He is not going to like it if he finds out that you lost that earring. For you there is only one way out—the bulletin board. So, at night, you creep along the empty streets, carrying a claw-hammer and a box of carpet tacks. Here is what you post up for all to read, "Lost: Sea Shell Earring between York Theatre and Porter's Avenue. Finder kindly return to...etc. Reward offered." Then you creep tremblingly home and hope for the best, before your boyfriend comes home and reads that notice.

After all, it is only the most retiring users of the bulletin board

"...the light in the window of the cottage..."

who see our town against the backdrop of an autumn night, when only the lights can tell their story. The illuminated dial of the post office clock points to midnight. Across the river, a motor car traces its way along the shore, then disappears around the point. At the mouth of the river, lighthouses send out warning and guidance to a big gypsum liner, moving in on the flood tide. Notice one of her lights winking? That's the first mate signalling to his wife; she lives in that little cottage over there on the river bank. Now the light in the window of the cottage is flashing on and off; she's answering him. Uptown, there is someone in the doctor's office. Nothing serious, just Doc putting away his hay fever pills and unpacking the flu tonics. He's just getting ready for winter. He will have all the customers he needs, and is one man who doesn't seem to have to advertise on our *Thumbtack Gazette*.

Belcher's Almanac

At about the turn of the century, a new textbook called *The Health Reader* was introduced into the Nova Scotia schools. The students in one school were advised by their teacher each to get one at the store. Next day, she made sure they all had a copy. One student, a little boy, did not. When the teacher inquired why he had not carried out her instructions, he said, "Well, Pa says I don't need *The Health Reader*. We have a copy of *Belcher's Almanac*."

I was told that as a true story, and I believe it too. Belcher's Almanac at one time occupied a place, in the Maritime provinces, somewhere between the Holy Bible and the Book of Common Prayer. Only with this difference—had *Belcher's Almanac* been in existence at the time of Noah, it would have predicted the flood a full year in advance.

"…occupied a place… somewhere between the Holy Bible and the Book of Common Prayer…"

Its most eagerly consulted pages were given over to weather prophecy. Today, with all the tools of science at his disposal, the weatherman finds it hard enough to predict the next 24 hours—but *Belcher* gave you the next 12 months! Is it any wonder that people treasured their almanac as if it contained the philosopher's stone? Even if a lot of it was guesswork, it allowed one to be so much in advance of one's neighbour. You knew when to cut your hay—and he didn't. He, poor soul, like the great majority a hundred years ago, probably did not even know how to read. It would be impossible for him to make use of all this wealth of thrilling information. You could find the railway schedule for the Halifax and South Western, fish and game laws, dates for every Sunday through the year, a form for making out your will, the fact that Minard's Linament is good for hair that is falling out....

The longest winter evenings passed quickly

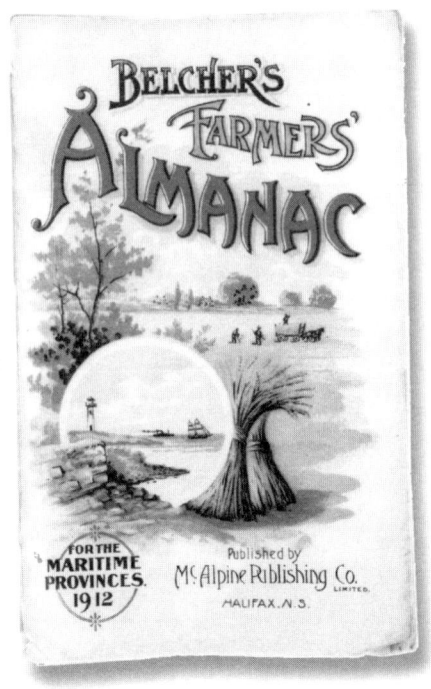

enough with facts like these to kindle the imagination. And if you felt like entertainment, pure and simple, there were jokes:

*Why is a talkative young man
like a young pig?
Because if he lives long enough,
he is likely to become a great bore.*

*What tables are most used
throughout the world?
Vegetables, eatables, and constables.*

A wag on hearing that a man had given up chimney sweeping expressed surprise as he thought the business sooted him.

All over the Maritimes, folk sat at their firesides, chuckling over these little gems and hugging to themselves the fact that they knew what the weather was going to be on a certain day six months from now. This was the real drawing card, this feeling of being able to see the future, and even though the weather forecasts were often far astray, the readers of *Belcher's Almanac* continued to have faith.

"...they knew what the weather was going to be..."

These forecasts were for many years prepared by Jonathan McCully, one of the Fathers of Confederation, a member of the Howe Government, and at one time editor of the *Halifax Morning Chronicle*. One year, to vary the monotony, he predicted that on July 16 there would be a devastating hailstorm—and lo, it came to pass. From then on there could be no question, *Belcher's*, somehow or other, knew what was coming.

Belcher's was not the only almanac published in the Maritimes. Almanacs were published in New Brunswick and on Prince Edward Island, while a number were produced in Halifax, such as *Cunnabell's, Nugent's* and the *Provincial Wesleyan*, but none enjoyed the popular acclaim of *Belcher's Farmers' Almanac* which ran for over a hundred years. It last appeared in 1930.

An Annapolis Valley man, Clement Horton Belcher, started the almanac. He was born in the district of Cornwallis and came of Planter stock. He came to Halifax as a young man and bought out George Eaton, one of the two booksellers of the infant city, whose business was on Granville Street, directly opposite the Provincial Building. In 1824, he issued the first edition of his famous almanac, and from its very beginning it caught the public fancy.

Belcher was at first not too happy about the weather predictions which he adopted with reluctance, for it disturbed him to see the public placing so much faith in something that had no substantial foundation but was merely guesswork. One year he abandoned the weather prophecies altogether. That year sales dropped off so abruptly that he was finally satisfied that his customers wanted the weather predictions—guesswork or otherwise—and, bowing to public demand, he reinstated them.

During a period of mild weather in the winter of 1830, an old farmer called to return his copy of the almanac and get his money back. He was highly annoyed that he had been misled into expecting snow. He had made arrangements for sleighing and sledding but the snow had not come. He opened up the almanac and pointed out these words which referred to a period of two or three weeks: "Look for snow about now," was the warning.

"So," said Mr. Belcher, "you say that you have been greatly disappointed."

"Yes," said the old farmer, "I've been waiting for snow these three weeks. Everybody has been lookin' for it and wonderin' why it don't come. The gals have lost out on their sleigh ride, and neighbour Goodwill says we shan't get our wood out at this rate." It looked as if Mr. Belcher was in a tight spot.

"I'm sorry," he said, "for your disappointment, but the fault is yours, and not the almanac's. If you will examine it again you will see that the almanac does not predict the *coming* of snow, but merely the *looking for* it. If snow had actually come, people would not have been looking for it, as you say everybody has been, even as foretold. Thus the prediction is verified." This logic so convinced the old farmer that he went away not only satisfied, but a firmer believer than ever before.

Farmers were not the only ones who swore by this book. Around the Bay of Fundy there was a saying among mariners that all you needed to be the captain of a coastal vessel was an alarm clock, a sounding lead, and a copy of *Belcher's Almanac*.

Belcher's not only included the tide tables for Saint John, but also listed every lighthouse, beacon, and bell buoy from Fort Folly Point to Briar Island. It told you what to look for—how many flashes a minute, the colour of the light and how far it was visible. In thick fog, you counted the number of blasts from the foghorn. It was all there.

Today, we know what the weather is going to be tomorrow, but in those wonderful far-off days of *Belcher's Almanac*, you could scan the future and spy a thundercloud eight months away—and learn when to plant your beans into the bargain. I don't know why they ever stopped publishing that book....

Fences

Beyond this cramping gray
Is the ripple of field and tree
Where breezes lightly play
And the dance of spring runs free.

Not knowing of fences or rust,
A trivial butterfly
Leaves withering yards and dust
For a height of calling sky.

Unstirring, the poet waits,
Enclosed and darkly forlorn—
To go suddenly through gates
With freedom, music-borne.

Alan Creighton

Fireplaces—And What They Tell Us

Yesterday, [in 1981] while shopping at our supermarket, I came on something I had never seen before. It was a novelty, a roast of beef weighing two pounds, two ounces. I was always under the impression that anything under four pounds in a roast was not worth bothering with, but it now appears that our ovens—or perhaps our pocketbooks—are somehow getting smaller. If prices keep going up, no doubt we'll be offered a roast of beef weighing exactly one pound, if such a thing is possible.

I cannot ever recall, even twenty years ago, seeing these midget-sized roasts in the meat cooler. But at that time, roasts of beef could be afforded by all of us. Nowadays many of us are stopping to reconsider, and turning instead to the hamburger department.

"...a house once known as Sangster's Inn, in Upper Falmouth..." Original watercolour by Cheryl Rutledge, Falmouth, NS.

The strange thing about all this is that we seem so much better off than we were twenty years ago. And, if you go back even further, most of our grandparents and great-grandparents were (if you can believe the record) practically starving to death.

For example, in the year 1852 in the village of Wallace, in Cumberland County, money was so scarce that the church elders did not think it wise to attempt to take up collections at Sunday services.

It was not only at Wallace. From all three Maritime provinces, you find evidence of whole communities which had virtually nothing in the way of hard cash. So that we, today, applying these facts in terms of the checkout counter, must conclude that these people lived in a state of gaunt and perpetual hunger. But was it really that bad? If nothing had come down to us but these chilling statistics of penury, we would have to imagine our ancestors teetering on the brink of starvation.

Something, however, has come down to us which offers a somewhat contradictory picture. It is not mere hearsay, but what we can see in our many century farms and older homes throughout the Maritimes—the solid and massive testimony of the chimneys and fireplaces of an earlier, and in many ways more abundant, age.

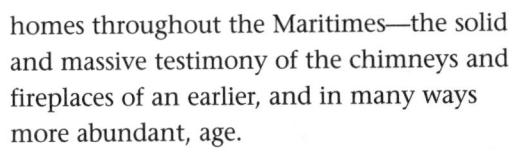

In a house once known as Sangster's Inn, in Upper Falmouth, Hants County, is a huge fireplace in the kitchen, which has a bakery oven large enough to hold twelve loaves and seventeen pies...at the same time. Anyone who stopped in at Sangster's Inn was certainly not going to starve.

They knew how to build kitchens in those days, and fireplaces too. Some homes had a fireplace so big that a man of quite normal height could walk inside it without bumping his head. Many old fireplaces had a crossbeam from which steaming pots were suspended over the fire and from which large roasts could be hung.

In some houses, you can still see the stone fireplaces, brick baking ovens, and hand-hewn timbers. The evidence is there for us to exam-

"They knew how to build kitchens in those days and fireplaces too."

ine, not dry facts and figures, but something you can look at. Run your hand over the globe-shaped iron pots of such ample proportions, and the andirons ready to support great logs. These hearths tell us a story, not of niggling economies but of warming abundance.

You catch this feeling of generous hospitality at Granville Ferry in the house known as North Hills, once the home of Robert Patterson who bequeathed it and its contents to the Nova Scotia Museum. It is now maintained as a fine example of the English Georgian period. The massive chimneys and fireplaces here are among the earliest in the province. On one of the beams is carved the date, 1702.

Annapolis Royal, of course, has many fine old fireplaces including examples of the hob fireplace. On Lower St. George Street is the Bailey House, once a boarding house operated by Mrs. Bailey. She was known to Sam Slick (and his creator, Thomas Haliburton) as Marm Bailey. In the ample fireplace, she prepared a delicacy known as moose muffle soup—the muffle being the projecting and prominent upper lip or nose of the moose. Marm Bailey's moose muffle soup became so popular that she developed quite a business, exporting it to England. Here, in case you should happen to come by a moose muffle, is her recipe. After simmering the moose muffle for the best part of an hour, she added a knuckle of veal, onions, thyme, marjoram, clove, cayenne, salt, force-meat balls fried in butter, tomato catsup, the yolks of twelve hard-boiled eggs, and lastly, a bottle of old port.

Moose muffle soup is something you *can't* buy in the supermarket.

"...a boarding house operated by Mrs. Bailey."

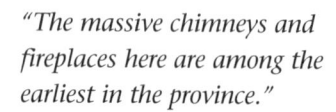

"The massive chimneys and fireplaces here are among the earliest in the province."

The Front Door Key—And Security

The great magician, Harry Houdini, was famous for his escapes from bondage. He would arrive in a city and invite the local police to tie him up and snap a pair of handcuffs on his wrists. Then he would allow himself to be submersed in a tank of water or some such impossible situation and, within a minute or so, he would be free. I doubt if he could get away with these tricks today. Padlocks and handcuffs have become far too sophisticated.

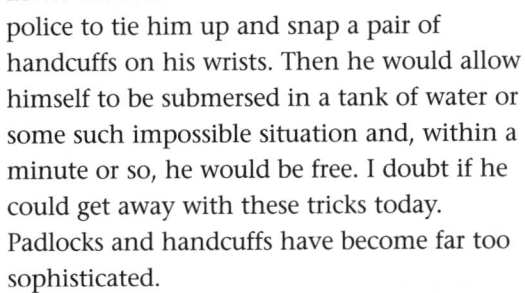

We've come a long way from the massive old locks and keys of yesteryear that tended to make up in size and beauty for what they lacked in security.

You'll see a fine example of this type of lock not too many miles from Wolfville, at the Prescott House at Starrs Point. This Georgian mansion has its front door locked with a brass key, which is twelve inches long.

Two or three miles from the Prescott House, at Town Plot, is an even earlier structure, built as barracks for officers of the militia. The sturdy key and heavy wrought-iron padlock for this building were placed on this officers' barracks in 1770. The key and padlock later came into the possession of Miss Rose Tobin of Town Plot who sold it, in 1927, to Mrs. W.M.P. Webster of Halifax, an enthusiastic collector of keys and antique locks.

At Annapolis Royal, you'll see the original key to the main gate of historic Fort Anne—a key that is nine inches long and weighs between two and three pounds. It was carried off to Boston in 1710 by a triumphant Colonel Nicholson, but was returned to the fort in 1922 as a gesture of international good will.

Now all these early locks and keys are impressive because only wealthy men could afford them. In fact, in the early days, we here in the Maritimes were not so much concerned about keeping *people* out. What bothered us was how to protect ourselves from the forces of evil. Here the lock and key were quite ineffective. You turned to something more powerful. Hence, in such places as Kings County, you find many fine examples of what is known as the Christian door, so called because the panels form a cross. This is a practice that comes down to us from medieval times, when such devices were used to keep out evil spirits.

Old Postcards

Although other parts of Canada seem to have been discovered by tourists many years ago, it seems that the Maritimes were overlooked until comparatively recently. During the 20s and 30s, nobody ever thought of coming here except for a few hunters in the fall. Most of the summertime visitors were *really* not visitors. They were people who had been born right here, coming home in vacation time to freeload on the old folks. I am wondering if, possibly, I may have stumbled on the explanation for the slow start to our tourism industry.

A few days ago, a neighbour of mine lent me a collection of old postcards which had belonged to his mother. They were cards that had been sent to her or other members of her family from friends, mostly in other parts of the Maritimes. The earliest cards are postmarked around the year 1900, and most of them were sent during the next ten or fifteen years, up to the time of the the First World War.

"...a collection of old postcards..."

As any of you know who have gone out to buy postcards recently, the cards being sold today are eye-catching masterpieces of colour photography. They show our beautiful province in the most flattering light, almost like travel bureau literature. You know the kind of thing. There are all these regional clichés; the yoke of white-faced oxen, the old red barn with lupins, the apple orchards, the smiling fishermen. These are all for the benefit of the would-be tourists. For the local population, most of these items have long since grown tiresomely repetitious and ho-hum.

However, the beguiling scene is not what you find on these old postcards. On the contrary, you have no idea to what lengths the photographers went to render the Maritimes in as modest and unexciting a context as possible. There are drab little back streets or an automobile, a model T, tootling along an unidentified straight road. Here is a picture of "Birch Street, Digby" which simply shows a street with a lot of trees. You can hardly see any houses; there are so many trees. You could send this to your friends in the States to show them what life was like on Digby's Birch Street; there is nobody there, just nothing but trees.

Here is a card showing a bit more action "On Main Street," somewhere. There is a sign suspended from a second storey window over a shop. "Big Sale," it says. "Shirts, Caps, Duck Coats." A woman walking on the opposite sidewalk seems to be on the point of crossing over, and away off down the street, a second customer is approaching by horse and buggy.

Another postcard shows "Granville Street, Bridgetown" on a sunny summer day. The street lies quiet under the elm trees. The shadow of a telephone pole cuts across the sidewalk outside the Western Union office. To think that shadow was made such a long time ago, as the photographer stood there with his tripod in the middle of the street. There is no traffic coming, so no worry about being run over. There is nobody in sight except a small boy in a straw hat. He is standing on the corner opposite the Grand Central Hotel, right beside the Union Bank of Halifax.

Here are some cards with a more thrilling motif. Many years ago, not far from where I live, there was a railway accident. A train went off the track and plowed into the mud. No one was killed but here were mail cars and express cars all over the mud flats. A local photographer saw this as a marvellous subject for a set of postcards. After all, it was a remarkable event for the people here in Hantsport and we felt that the world should know about it. For years we sent these postcards to our friends, showing them what they might expect in the way of transportation if they thought of coming on a visit.

Similar calamities were pictured in other towns; collapsing bridges, ships piled up on the rocks, devastating fires. We wanted our friends to know just how exciting life really could be in the Maritimes.

"Granville Street, Bridgetown, on a sunny summer day."

To offset these more sombre themes there were some postcards in a lighter vein. Here, for example, is one showing a young man saying goodbye to his wife. He is dressed like a dandy with a top hat, wing collar, and white tie with a tremendous yellow rose in his buttonhole. He is saying, "What, take you to Hot Springs—you are making it hot enough for me right here!"

This was the age of the suffragette and of prohibition. Women were making it hot for men in a number of ways. Here is a postcard entitled "Don't go Near the Bar Room, Brother." It shows a man on the point of entering a door marked "Spirits." He is rather sagging at the knees. A would-be Carrie Nation stands facing him, barring the way to the door. Her hand is extended. She has him by the shoulder and is saying,

Don't go near the bar room, brother
Shun it as an evil place.
Do not yield to its temptation
For it will bring you deep disgrace.
Friends and brothers all around you
Council you to pass it by.
Let the pleadings of your darling sister
Strengthen you once more to try.

This one is copyrighted in 1906 and was just the sort of card you could send to anyone who enjoyed an occasional glass of wine—to make them feel a little bit guilty.

No wonder we were ignored by the rest of the world for so long. With this sort of publicity we might have held the tourists off for another century. They were doing their best, those early photographers, back in the good old days....

"...a marvelous subject for a set of postcards."

WRECK NEAR HANTSPORT. TRANSFERRING PASSENGERS

Hazards of Larceny

In London, England, the tourists, many of them Canadians, have been doing so much shoplifting that the authorities are now issuing pamphlets warning the visitor of the risk he runs. Getting caught, as the pamphlet points out, is very embarrassing for all concerned. They want to help the tourist enjoy himself, but above all, they want him to avoid being caught.

To this same end, I would like to warn our own tourists of certain pitfalls, which should be avoided...if larceny is not to be an unpleasant experience.

First of all, don't steal anything you can't dispose of. In museums and archives, being light-fingered among the exhibits of broadswords and antique fowling-pieces can be extremely hazardous, not because you'll be nabbed by the museum guards—most of the time there's nobody around. You can probably slip a duelling rapier down your trouser leg and walk a little stiffly, but once out of the building, what do you do with the thing?

"...the soup dishes filled with silver..."

Dealers all across the country have an alert system of their own. If you try to sell the rapier to them they'll first make sure of your identity, then quietly phone the museum because they have special ways of spotting artifacts that originate in museums.

If you go in for robbing the till, watch your step! Some years ago, a break-and-enter artist began preying on the merchants in several Annapolis Valley towns. His specialty was small change, which he figured could never be traced. Every week or so, for the best part of a year, the canvas bags of quarters and dimes would be missing from some restaurant or movie house. The police could get nowhere; not a single clue had been left.

Then one day, at a grocery story on Main Street, the driver of a milk truck stopped in to ask if he could get some folding money in exchange for silver. One of his customers had bought a month's supply of milk tickets and paid for them with silver—several soup plates just filled with nickles and dimes....

It so happened that the town policeman was in the store at the time this exchange took place. He began drawing conclusions. Later, when the Mounties called at the home of this man with all the soup dishes filled with silver, they found bean crocks and roasting pans overflowing with quarters and dimes, a cornucopia of small change which ultimately led to the prisoner's dock. So, don't use all that silver to buy milk tickets—or anything else. Someone might be watching.

In Annapolis Royal, along St. George Street, next to the old Queen Hotel, there used to be a tavern, well patronized by soldiers stationed at Fort Anne. It was run by a Mrs. Reynolds. One day, after hours, when the tavern was closed, one of the soldiers developed a great thirst for a pint of beer. He decided the only way to get it was to enter the tavern by way of the chimney. It was one of those vast old-fashioned chimneys, but what the soldier didn't realize was that the chimney was divided into two parts, one descending to the open fireplace in the public tavern, the other providing a flue for the kitchen stove. In the excitement of his descent, he took the wrong turning and got jammed in the flue just as the family fire was being lighted.

Luckily for him, his cries for help were heard downstairs. Someone climbed up on the roof and a rope was lowered. The slightly singed solider was removed from the chimney and, rumour has it, he did get a cooling draught of ale.

All the same, chimneys are not recommended for breaking and entering.

The Cord Saver

Let's see what kind of a person you are. Suppose you have arrived home from the post office, carrying a big parcel done up in brown wrapping paper, secured and tied with heavy cord, well knotted—a parcel from the mail order house. You set it on the dining room table. The family all gather about, waiting for the parcel to be opened.

Now, you will prove what manner of man you are. Do you cut the cord? Or do you untie the knots?

If, holding fast to your principles, you grapple with the knot, brushing aside proffered scissors and eager pen-knives, then there can be no question. You are a member of that vanishing race, the cord saver, who exists today as a throwback to an age when thrift was a virtue, to that bygone time when people hearkened to the counsel of *Poor Richard's Almanac*: "A penny saved is a penny earned."

A vanishing race, did I say? I'm not so sure about that. I feel somehow that here, in Canada's Maritime provinces, there are still quite a lot of cord savers around, and paper bag hoarders, and those who set great store by an empty marmalade jar....

Now, what you must understand is that there is nothing mean or common about these people, the true cord savers. I am talking about the real thing now, not these pale imitations who accumulate a bare shoe-box of string; this is mere trifling and not worthy of the name. No, the true cord saver is moved by an instinct that is almost elemental in its intensity. He is a phenomenon, a natural force. He sweeps through life like some tropical tornado, sucking in worn-out window blinds, plastic bags, broken hot-plate elements, bottle caps, used typewriter ribbons, and the tinfoil that comes in cigarette packages. It is all grist to a mill that never runs, for none of this debris is ever put to use.

You see, a cord saver belongs to that rare species of man, the dreamer. He is only

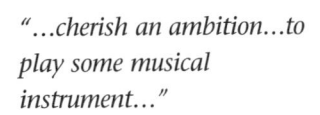

"...cherish an ambition...to play some musical instrument..."

reluctantly in touch with work-a-day reality, only long enough to snatch these precious items from the oblivion of the dustbin; then he is off soaring in a world of his own, furnished with fabulous collections of empty pickle bottles, rag-bags bulging with tattered sheets, long past patching, and ancient gramophone records which he never plays.

I have sometimes tried to understand the meaning of it all, this passion for collecting. I wonder if what we see here is only the frank and open display of what is happening secretly in a great many lives.

How many of us cherish an ambition to learn to play some musical instrument, some day, when we have the time. But, of course, the time never comes.

Here is a man who plans to take up mountain climbing after he retires. But he's forgetting something; by then, his knees may not be so flexible. So, I fancy, we all accumulate these dreams, these untried enthusiasms, much as the cord saver does.

There is something very heart-warming about these people, surrounded by their empty pickle bottles, their closets brimming over with paper bags and biscuit boxes filled with teapot lids from teapots long since smashed and gone. Perhaps they have found a use for these things, as they dream of another world where pickle bottles are never empty, where there is always a steeping fragrant teapot to fit every lid...and a parcel waiting to be wrapped and tied with cord.

"...biscuit boxes filled with teapot lids..."

PATCHES

When I was a boy, a patch on your trousers was like the insignia of manhood—a Distinguished Service Cross worn on the knee—to commemorate night raids on Astrakhan apple trees, insurmountable barbed-wire fences, and obstreperous schoolyard scuffles. A patch was an emblem of accomplishments and a mark of good housewifery. The mothers who sewed those patches on took pains to tuck the edges in, to match the material. They vied with their neighbours in producing examples of fine needlework. A patch, a good patch, was a source of pride.

But things have changed. Not long ago, a neighbour of mine undertook to put a patch in the knee of her son's trousers. He is in grade three. When she handed the trousers back to him, he refused to wear them. Patched trousers were simply unthinkable, he explained to her. Well, she phoned his teacher and his teacher agreed with the boy; there wasn't one boy in school, she said, with a patch in his trousers. If any boy did turn up wearing a patch, she felt he would be given a pretty rough time of it by the rest of the class. She advised the mother to buy him a new pair of trousers.

What has happened to us? Something has been happening that affects our whole outlook on life. We are no longer interested in "making do." We don't treasure things the way we used to. The whole concept of remaining content with what we have is being rejected. This reflects, of course, our general prosperity but it goes even deeper than that. Science has infected us all with a great dissatisfaction. Across our skies the jets are writing a manifesto of miracles yet to come. Against their streaming banners the idea of patching one's clothes, of putting up with anything that's frumpish or old-fashioned, seems ludicrously out-of-place. So, I suppose, it's only natural that we should be raising our eyes to the stars, to a vision of a world that is youthful, vibrant, free, and forever new—new and exciting.

Nobody likes having old stuff around the house any more. Even old *people* are something of a bore these days. So we build homes for them that are prodigies of up-to-dateness, with the last word in plumbing and kitchen fixtures, the kind of modern push-button kitchen that is just bound to make grandma feel at home.

We have new fabrics, new foods, new detergents. Have you noticed how frequently that word *new* is being used? It doesn't really mean new, you know; it means more desirable.

Advertisers have equated the idea of newness with improvement, with progress. Anything new, it follows, is bound to be better.

Take the matter of shoes. We used to have a shoemaker in our town, a cobbler, a man who sat on a leather-padded bench, examined our shoes and decided if the uppers were sound enough to sustain a new set of half-soles. But not any more. He has moved away to a bigger town. There is not the business here now to support a shoemaker. Shoes nowadays—are meant to be worn out and thrown away.

But then shoes don't wear out nearly as fast as they used to because nobody walks any more. Walking used to be looked on as a quite respectable way of keeping in shape. Instead of walking, we now make a big production out of this brand new business of exercise. There are books on it, books full of pictures of you standing on your head, and doing fifty push-ups, and being madly full of energy. You can get a set of gramophone records that'll keep you busy doing knee bends until you get tired and turn the thing off. Yes, you can take exercise right in your own home, without bothering to go for a walk.

"...a cobbler...decided if the uppers were sound enough to sustain a new set of half soles."

If you've grown a little puffy and short in the wind from watching TV and always driving to work, why not subscribe to this course in yoga? It will explain to you how to breathe and take care of the years of paunchy neglect.

Dreams are so much more fun than the tedious reality of having to look after things like oiling the washing machine, painting the window screens, tightening a door knob—a patch here, a patch there, with its unwelcome reminder that we're not as young as we used to be. But sometimes it has its disadvantages, this dream-world refusal to deal with things in practical, down-to-earth terms. I saw an example of this recently that came very close to being a dreadful tragedy.

Near the town where I live is a bridge over a little river. It is a one-lane bridge, which is perfectly all right as long as everyone knows it's a one-lane bridge. The local people have no trouble at all. They know it is impossible for two cars to pass on the bridge, so they graciously give way to the car that reaches the bridge first. No problems.

But when strangers come speeding toward you, then watch out. On the side of the road, close by, the highway department has placed a neat little sign, telling that it is a one-lane bridge—but most people approaching at sixty miles an hour would scarcely give it a glance.

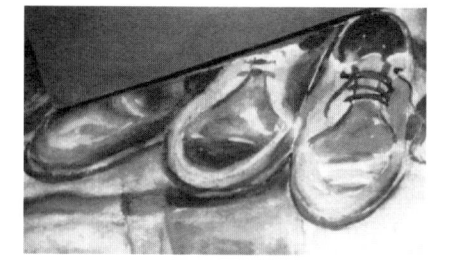

What is needed is a sign at each end of the bridge, on the bridge itself, forming a portal that one must pass under—a sign ten feet high, in flaming letters of gold, lit up at night like Times Square on New Year's Eve....Just one word, one simple word—DANGER—would do the trick. Then they would stop; then they would wait; then they would give way to the other car.

But now, there is not a word of warning on the bridge and my doctor tells me a quite horrifying story of the number of cases he has treated this year of people cut and crippled in head-on collisions on that one-lane bridge.

In a recent collision between a truck and a touring car, the three passengers in the touring car were hauled to safety only moments before the car burst into flames—all because there was no sign on the bridge. Why wasn't there a sign on the bridge? You give a guess. My guess is that the word *danger* on that bridge would stand out like an ugly patch and we don't like patches nowadays. It would remind us uneasily that the bridge was not quite as modern as some other bridges. We like to think of ourselves as being up-to-date, we don't like presenting a poor image to the tourists. So, rather than warn them properly, we go without the patch...and keep on having accidents.

The reaction of people around here, of course, is one of impatience with the highway department. They say, "It's a disgrace! Should be torn down! It's time that old bridge was replaced with one wide enough to allow traffic to pass." But I don't agree. As far as I can see, the bridge is perfectly sound....All it needs—is a patch.

"...everyone knows it's a one-lane bridge..."

Every Night at Seven

If you live in a little country town, as I do, you will understand how we feel about gangster pictures. We don't approve of them. We think they are a menace. Some of us even speak of a boycott. Yet we never miss one of them. We daren't....we have to go; otherwise the theatre would be out of business.

You see, our town has a population of barely fourteen hundred; it is just big enough to support the one movie house. So a boycott is out of the question. If the movie house closed down, the town would not seem the same at all. I don't know what we would do if there were no show to go to.

I say movie house, but actually it shares the building with the Masonic and IOOF lodge rooms upstairs. There are no matinées except on Saturdays, but, every night at seven, some of us are drawn like moths to the warm glow of the red-and-green neon sign.

EMPIRE THEATRE AT HANTSPORT OPENS MONDAY Oct 30 1939

Fitted out with complete duplicate projection and sound equipment, as up to date as that of any town theatre in the province the old "Empire" Theatre at Hantsport will open on Monday with "The Rage of Paris."

J. H. Bustin, manager of Imperial Theatre, Windsor, has taken a lease of the Empire to give residents of Hantsport the same community entertainment advantages as enjoyed by other towns, and Hantsport, one time known...

"...our town...is just big enough to support the one movie house."

You can't miss it. It is in plain view of the post office. So, when you've discovered that there are no letters on the evening train, well, you can always drown your disappointment by stepping over to the theatre to see what Humphrey Bogart is up to.

The prosperity of our movie house is a matter of lively concern to all of us. In its ups and downs, we see the industrial life of our town reflected. When times are thriving, you can count as many as two dozen cars parked outside. By five minutes to seven there is a regular queue waiting at the box office. No one is the least impatient; quite the contrary, we love to have to line up. It means that the pulp mill is working full time. There's money to spend. Everyone is happy and laughing, standing there waiting to buy a ticket.

That is when business is booming. But it is not a full house every night, oh dear no! So many things affect our theatre. Take the weather now. The effect of dry sunny weather can be almost calamitous. Last spring, for example, we had a long spell of drought. The

"...no matinées, except on Saturdays..."

lakes went down, hydro plants were unable to turn out enough power and, consequently, the pulp mill operated only part time. So a big feature production like Ray Milland in *So Evil My Love* met strong opposition in the counter attraction, So Large My Grocery Bill. Even Judy Garland is spurned for a pound of T-bone steak. All this because of the weather.

In the evenings, you would see our theatre manager standing under the neon sign, anxiously scanning the sky for thunder clouds. Inside, the regular patrons whispered nervously among themselves,

"Doesn't look like he'll have a paying house tonight."

"Think there'll be any for the second show?"

"Might be if the Town Council gets out early."

I can tell you it was a pretty anxious time for all of us. In two weeks time we were to have a picture starring Rita Hayworth, but would the theatre still be open by then? The skies continued sunny, and the outlook dark. Then, finally the heavens opened and almost drowned out our first of July street parade. Everyone was jubilant—we got to see Rita Hayworth after all.

If a man knows how to run a small-town movie house, he has solved about all the problems in the entertainment world. Look what he is up against. In the winter it's hockey. On the night when our town plays Kentville, you have to show a "revealing" picture like *Mom and Dad*, otherwise there wouldn't be a teenager left in town. As for the springtime, Hollywood has yet to produce a film to compare with our Apple Blossom Festival. Then, later on, during summer, what with moonlight beach parties and the Wednesday night band concert at the Community Centre grounds, not to mention bingo and baseball, you can imagine what a skilful choice of pictures it takes to keep anyone in the theatre.

In the autumn, when the ladies of the Anglican Sanctuary Guild announce a special supper of hot mulligatawny stew, to be served at eight o'clock in the evening...you have to bring up your big guns for something like that—something like Jane Russell in *The Outlaw*.

The other day I was in Halifax and, having some time to kill, I took in a movie. It was at a brand new picture house, supposed to have the latest word in acoustics. I never was so disappointed in all my born days. They had gone to work and soundproofed the place! All you heard was what was on the screen. A small-town movie theatre wouldn't make a mistake like that.

Suppose Bing Crosby is just starting to sing "I'm Dreaming of a White Christmas," when, all of a sudden, the siren over at the Town Hall begins its long crescendo of alarm, does anybody feel annoyed? Certainly not. If there is a fire in town, we want to know about it. All over the darkened hall, members of the Voluntary Fire Brigade are getting up and groping their way out to the lobby. In a few minutes you hear the hose-truck backing out of the Fire Hall, its siren wails off in the direction of Main Street, and we know our town is safe.

Soundproofing....Who ever heard of such an idea! Why, in summertime, all the doors are left open for ventilation. The blue curtains under the red exit lights sway in the draught of a warm August evening and you catch the voices and laughter of the young people passing by on the sidewalk.

I wonder if you saw the movie version of *Green Dolphin Street*? You did? Oh, what a pity. Remember the earthquake? It was one of the finest things Hollywood ever did. Only, in our town, Hollywood did not do it—not the best part of it anyway. We added the final touch of realism ourselves.

Trees were crashing to the ground, the earth was cracking open, houses were crumbling like matchwood....That was where we took over....For us alone, the rumbling grew louder, then the floor began to shake....For earthquake effects, you can't beat a passing freight train. You see our movie house is right alongside the railway track. And some people believe in soundproofing!

I seem to be talking about pictures you saw several years ago? Well naturally. These are the only kind we bother with—productions that have stood the test of time. Like old friends and old wine, a good film gathers flavour to itself with age. When Mr. Belvedere begins his babysitting on our screen, we seem to catch the echo of a nation's laughter. We do not mind being three years late. He who laughs last laughs best, you know.

All this encourages a more leisurely approach to the events of the day. In real life, current history moves with the speed of a rocket ship; but as it emerges from our projection room, time is mercifully delayed. One's lagging brain is given a chance to catch up with what is going on in the world. At the close of the war, we saw Hitler marching into Paris. By 1945, we were storming the beaches at Midway and Guadalcanal. Only last winter [1949] we dropped the bomb on Hiroshima. From now on, we can look forward to several years of peace.

Now, let's take our eyes off the picture for a moment and examine the audience which is really far more interesting than anything on the screen. In our theatre, the audience can be divided into two groups: those who believe in sitting in the middle section and those who like to sit in the side sections next to the wall. Of course, everyone is united in not wanting to sit on the hard wooden seats up front. These first seven rows are provided, I believe, as a sort of penance for anyone who arrives late, after the good seats—the leather cushioned ones—are all taken. I may say that the hard seats do seem to have a special attraction for the youngsters. They prefer the front row, where they can aim their pea-shooters directly at the close-ups of Dorothy Lamour.

"For earthquake effects, you can't beat a passing freight train."

But to return to the good seats. These are covered in brown leather, and the padding is so full and luxurious that, when you sit down, there is a squishing sound. Why there are side sitters and middle sitters, I do not know exactly. It may be a matter of conviction or of family habit.

Suppose the son of a family that has always sat in the seats on the left-hand side, one evening looks across the aisle at a girl sitting in the middle section...and she becomes his wife....When they come to the movies after their marriage, we all watch to see whether they sit on the left-hand side or in the middle. Then we'll know who is the boss in that family.

We all share a common affection for the stage of our theatre, for those footlights hold a memory for all of us. We've all been up there, perhaps as kiddies in the Christmas pantomime, or maybe it was at the sacred concert on a Sunday night, when we sang in the massed choir. Then there was the minstrel show....And, at the end of June, the stage is banked up high with flowers and the girls are all wearing white dresses and a yellow rose. The boys and girls are called up onto the stage to receive their diplomas and prizes. That is a night you will always remember—the High School graduation.

Well, it must be about time to turn on the house lights, open the exit doors, and leave our local theatre. I hope there is one just like it in your neighbourhood.

"...we all watch to see whether they sit on the left-hand side or in the middle."

Postscript

> Times have changed...
> And yet...as I look back...it strikes me that Hantsport...
> and the surrounding country...remains very much today...
> what it always was...

From a 1986 letter to Bishop Arnold, typed by Norman Creighton.

Index of Nova Scotia Place Names

Amherst 126
Annapolis County 35
Annapolis River 8, 53, 64, 104
Annapolis Royal 8, 34, 35, 53-56, 57, 65, 104, 107, 109, 132, 137, 139, 167, 169, 174
Antigonish 126
Auburn 133, 134, 140
Avonport 12, 18
Avon River 3, 9-14, 16, 18, 19, 27, 96
Aylesford 8, 139
Bedford 2
Berwick 63, 100, 126
Big Cove 119
Blue Beach 13
Boot Island 13
Briar Island 124, 164
Bridgetown 33, 50-52, 64, 65, 93, 104, 132, 140, 171
Canning 96
Cape Blomidon 3, 8, 14, 15, 38, 57, 62, 80, 81
Cape Breton 77, 89, 90, 91, 106, 126
Cape Sable Island 90, 96
Cape Sharp 80, 81
Card Beach 14, 19
Carleton's Corner 132
Castle Frederick 89-91
Centreville (Digby Neck) 115
Centreville (Kings County) 64
Cogmagun River 13

Colchester County 91
Cornwallis 32, 33, 63, 64, 92, 163
Cornwallis River 83
Cumberland County 166
Dartmouth 126
Digby 8, 59, 111, 115, 119, 124, 125, 134, 139, 141, 142, 171
Digby Neck 8, 58, 114, 115
Eldridge Settlement 36
Falmouth 8, 14, 19, 89-91, 166, 167
French Shore 58
Gaspereau 71
Gaspereau River 8, 18
Grand Pré 8, 18, 32, 40, 60, 69-72
Granville Ferry 34, 35, 38, 53, 54, 107-109, 115, 167
Greenwich 79
Greenwood 32
Gullen's Brook 36
Gulliver's Cove 115
Halfway River (Parrsboro) 79-81
Halifax 3, 4, 5, 11, 12, 32, 47, 52, 73, 80, 81, 83, 84, 90, 91, 102, 114, 116, 118, 125, 127, 128, 135, 138, 140, 162, 163, 169, 171, 182
Halls Harbour 85, 86
Hants County 96
Hantsport 2, 4, 5, 8, 11, 13, 16, 17, 21-23, 32, 33, 36, 73, 75, 76, 125, 126, 128, 131, 149, 171, 172, 179, 180, 185

Horton 18, 63, 80
Horton Bluff 12, 14, 73
Hortonville 18
Kejimkujik Lake 35
Kennetcook River 13
Kentville 4, 18, 33, 65, 96, 121, 138, 141, 182
Kings County 83, 96, 141, 169
Kingsport 14
Lake Rossignol 118
Lakeville 96
Little River 116
Long Island 69
Long Lake 11
Louisbourg 89, 109
Lunenburg 29
Lunenburg County 97
Mahone Bay 29
Margaretsville 48, 49
Melanson 71
Michener Point 14
Middleton 47, 119
Mill Village 127
Minudie 91
Mount Denson 19
Mount Shubel 116
New Minas 141
Newport Landing 96
Noggin Corner (Greenwich) 79-81
North Mountain 8, 31, 38, 54
Parkers Cove 54
Parrsboro 14, 79-81
Peggy's Cove 57
Port George 48
Port Lorne 48
Port Williams 83, 84, 132
Queens County 35

Rose Bay 97
St. Peters 126
Sandy Cove 8, 57-60, 114-116
Scots Bay 57, 80
Sheet Harbour 126
Smiths Cove 124
South Shore 10, 29
Starrs Point 169
Summerville 3, 10, 14
Sydney 90
Terry's Creek (Port Williams) 83
Three Lakes 11
Town Plot (Port Williams) 83, 169
Truro 80, 109
Vaughan 11
Wallace 166
Welsford 100, 103
Westphal 75
Weymouth 58, 110-112
Willow Brook 2
Wilmot 46
Wilmot Springs 46-49
Windsor 8, 13, 17, 34, 80, 89, 90, 98, 99, 111, 126, 127, 128
Windsor Forks 12,
Windsor Junction 139
Wolfville 8, 43-45, 60, 69, 79, 137, 169
Wreck Cove 106
Yarmouth 58, 103, 138, 143